HANGING ONTO
THE AMERICAN DREAM

HANGING ONTO THE AMERICAN DREAM

*A Story of Business Leadership
and Leaving a Legacy*

by
Susan Wilson Solovic

TABLE OF CONTENTS

Dedication   *III*

Acknowledgements   *V*

Preface   *VII*

Introduction   *IX*

One   *Leaders Learn Through Life Experiences*   *1*

Two   *Leaders Take Risks*   *15*

Three *Surviving the War Years*   *27*

Four   *Leading Into a New Era*   *41*

Five   *Lee/Rowan: Where the World Gets Organized*   *51*

Six   *Leaders Bring Style and Substance*   *67*

Seven *Transitions*   *75*

Eight *Leaders are Benevolent*   *83*

Nine   *The Collaborative Vision*   *95*

Ten   *Building on Success*   *113*

Eleven *Leaders Leave Their Mark on the World*   *147*

Twelve *In His Own Words*   *155*

Prologue   *157*

E. Desmond Lee & James P. Rowan, Founders of Lee/Rowan

DEDICATION

To my wife Mary Ann and in memory of my first wife, the late Margery Stauffer Lee.

To my children, Gayle, Gary and Christy and my grandchildren, Elizabeth and David Lee, Lyrica Marquez and Desmond Duggan; Mary Ann's children, Andrew Taylor and Jo Ann Kindle; Mary Ann's grandchildren, Kelly, Patty and Chrissy Taylor, Allison and Carolyn Kindle.

In recognition of my long-time friend and fellow founder of Lee/Rowan, James P. Rowan.

Lee/Rowan Company Logo

Acknowledgements

I t is my hope that the contents of this book will be a reflection of a journey of transition for the betterment of our community. I thank my friend Robert Hermann, who suggested this book be written.

May the present staff of professors, collaborating organizations and institutions who uphold our vision be an example for present and future individuals with the same spirit and commitment.

While it is extremely difficult to single out any individual who has been the most influential in my life during my second career, I would like to mention two: Dr. Blanche Touhill, Chancellor Emeritus of the University of Missouri-Saint Louis; Dr. William Danforth, Chancellor/Chairman Emeritus of Washington University.

These two people have many qualities in common. They are highly intelligent, visionary, creative, persevering, determined, analytical and they have fine judgment. They are caring and loving and devoted servants of their respective universities.

These people have inspired me to reach beyond myself, not only in generosity, but in spirit. I am indebted to them for collaborating with me for the enrichment of this community.

Des Lee

UM St. Louis

THE MAGAZINE OF THE UNIVERSITY OF MISSOURI-ST. LOUIS ❦ FALL 2003

Des Lee's Vision

Leads to a Framework of Collaboration

DES LEE AND HIS ENDOWED PROFESSORS

PREFACE

e smiles warmly with humility that belies the essence of the man he is. Those who knew him as an insecure child growing up in central Missouri would scarcely recognize him today. His success in business is refreshing in a world tainted by infectious greed and corporate malfeasance.

This is a story about personal challenges, business risks and rewards, leadership, integrity, vision, success and giving back. It is one man's story, but it is a story that imparts valuable lessons that serve as a primer for today's business leaders.

It is a story of the American Dream. It is the story of E. Desmond Lee.

E. Desmond Lee

INTRODUCTION

"We must never lose hope in trying to better the lives of people around us so that they may radiate the message to others."

– E. Desmond Lee

Surrounded by friends, family, business associates and admirers, E. Desmond Lee confidently strides to the podium amid a backdrop of thunderous applause. Tonight he is the recipient of the 1996 Man-Of-The-Year Award in Saint Louis, Missouri. For a man who claims he flunked kindergarten, this is quite an accomplishment. And he often asks with a look of bewilderment on his face, "Why would they pick me for this award? I'm just a chicken s… wire bender."

He is referring to the business he founded in 1939 with his best friend Jim Rowan and both of their fathers. Their product: Trouser creasers and hangers. Their success – undeniable. The company weathered the Depression, World War II, post-war booms and busts, evolving markets, encroaching global competition and technological advancements. From a fledgling start-up housed in a ramshackle $10-a-month quarters, the company became an international industry leader in the home storage equipment market reaching, $130 million in revenue.

As the company grew, so did competitive challenges and Des Lee made the difficult decision to sell the family business in 1993 – a decision that lined his pockets with gold.

"The day the check came through for the sale made payable to Des, the bank said that was the largest single check to an individual they had ever seen," says Carole Ritter, Des' longtime executive assistant.

Unwilling to retire like most of his contemporaries, Des began to look for something to do with the second chapter of his life. He developed an innovative plan to give his money back to the community.

Life experiences have caused Des to look beyond himself and his financially comfortable existence into a world of discrimination as well as freedom; of suffering as well as ease; and of limitations as well as far horizons. He wanted to make a difference and effect change. So he founded the Des Lee Collaborative Vision: Connecting Saint Louis Through Educational & Community Partnerships at the University of Missouri-Saint Louis, Washington University and Webster University.

The program endows professors at three universities in Saint Louis, with the stipulation the professors agree to spend a significant amount of their time working within the community and collaborating with one another. To the best of his knowledge, Des believes there is no other program like it in the country.

Des' willingness to give back to the community has allowed him to leave legacies rivaled only by titans like Rockefeller, Kennedy, Gates and Hertz. His gifts will live on into perpetuity.

His charitable giving approaches $50 million. The April 1999 *Worth* magazine (a financial intelligence publication) ranked him 98th among the 100 "most generous Americans" – the only Saint Louisan and one of only two Missourians to make the list.

"President George Bush stated that any description of a successful person in today's world must include service to others," Des noted. "I don't know anything more rewarding for me than trying to help others. And I'm busy at it all the time," he adds.

In light of all he has done, there is little doubt why this gregarious business giant and compassionate philanthropist would be named man of the year in his hometown. There is also little doubt as to why a man of this magnitude would be the focus of a book.

Certainly, there are stories about great leaders, but in this day and age where far too many of our business leaders seek immediate gratification and their primary goal is to line their own pockets at the expense of their employees and shareholders, Des Lee is a case study in how to build an empire based on ingenuity, sweat and integrity and then spend his wealth to better the lives of society's underserved and often forgotten.

Des ignored nay-sayers and side-stepped adversity both personally and professionally. He is a blend of Tom Sawyer, Sam Walton, Bill Gates and Will Rogers. He appears to live without a care in the world – sauntering down to the corner drugstore for a friendly chat with his friends. And he has lots of those. To meet him is to feel that you are the most important person in his day, and you'll probably get a teasing compliment.

He frequently turned the tables to me, joking, "I ought to write this book about you. You're more interesting than I am. I don't know what you see in me." In fact, at the end of the day, he's not a fellow who's enthused about being the subject of a book. "Too damn egotistical and I don't need it," he says.

Typically, Des deflects compliments and doesn't take credit for his accomplishments. He is a man haunted by self-doubt, yet he doesn't let his worries show to the world. Today, he acts more like an easy-going fisherman on a sunny riverbank than a one-time corporate fighter.

Fiercely competitive with a soft heart and spine of steel, many say he is an entrepreneurial genius. To that comment he replies with his typical aw-shucks, country-boy charm, "I am not an entrepreneurial guru. I was just a co-founder of a midsize company in a niche business that survived for 54 years."

Wildly successful by any measure, it is his integrity, business acumen, and sincere focus on people that makes him an inspiration and a role model.

"I am just a guy who made hangers who gives money away to the community. I guess that's one of the unique things about me," Des explains.

Yes Des, it is unique. Getting to know this uncommon man while writing this book was both a privilege and a pleasure. He is a breath of fresh air in today's stale and smoke-filled business world. I have tried, perhaps feebly, to capture the greatness of this man, but mere words cannot describe his brilliance, his compassion, his unwavering authenticity or his vision. He is a man who deeply loves his family, his community and his country, and who, without question, would give you the shirt off his back.

Through the chapters of this book, which journey through the life of this astounding man, you'll not only discover secrets of true leadership, but you'll watch a company grow step-by-step through sheer perseverance and will power. Also, interspersed throughout are letters from satisfied customers that demonstrate the company not only talked the talk, it walked the walk. When was the last time one of your clients or customers wrote you a thank-you letter for your product or service? The lessons we can all learn from Des' story I hope will renew and revitalize our own sense of business values and establish guideposts based on honesty and sincere leadership.

HANGING ONTO
THE AMERICAN DREAM

Young Des Lee on the Campus of Christian College in Columbia, Missouri

Chapter One

Leaders Learn Through Life Experiences

"I am a great believer in the American Dream."

– Des Lee

In many ways, businesses are like children. Children learn values as they grow up and these values serve as the foundation for their character and future success. The same is true of businesses. The values a company adopts in its infancy create the basis for the ongoing culture of the organization. An organization that operates with unethical standards in the beginning cannot escape the consequences later in its existence. In order to build a strong company based on the guiding principles of integrity, the initial leadership must have an unwavering commitment to its core values every day of its existence.

As a child, Des Lee learned the importance of honesty, hard work, ingenuity, competitiveness, sportsmanship, a desire to learn and a general appreciation for people. In turn, he carried these values with him into the business world and they served as a beacon guiding his leadership style – during times of abundance as well as in adversity and challenge to his ultimate success.

****

Times were hard. The year was 1917. The war raged on across the Atlantic while Americans enjoyed an era of great prosperity. Prices were up but so were wages. Unemployment was virtually nonexistent. Puerto Rico became a U.S. territory and the world lost great ragtime pianist and composer Scott Joplin. The day the United States entered the war, April 6, 1917, composer George M. Cohan wrote "Over There" and British Prime Minister David Lloyd George said, "America has at one bound become a world power in a sense she never was before."

That was the world during the summer when the 35th U.S. President John F. Kennedy, former U.S. Supreme Court Justice Byron R. White, American blues singer Lena Horne, and successful entrepreneur and philanthropist Edgar Desmond Lee were born.

Des was a curious child. At the tender age of six months, he went off to college – and to an all girls school at that. Well, at least that's the way he likes to tell the story.

Des' father Edgar Lee was the superintendent of schools in Sikeston, Missouri. He relinquished that post to become a professor of history at Christian College – now known as Columbia College. Edgar Lee moved his wife Bennetta their six-year-old daughter Virginia and their baby boy Des to Columbia, Missouri. After several years, Edgar Lee was appointed president of the college.

LEADERS RECOGNIZE THE NEED FOR CHANGE AND LEARN TO ADAPT

"Leadership is about taking an organization to a place it would not have otherwise gone without you, in a value-adding, measurable way."

– George M.C. Fisher

Without strong leadership, organizations and institutions stagnate. They can't keep pace with changing markets, and as a result they eventually become extinct. True leaders are visionaries. Imagine being the buggy whip manufacturer who refused to recognize the rising popularity of the automobile and, as a result, failed to move with the times.

There is nothing more constant than change in any business environment – particularly in today's markets. Successful companies embrace change and they learn to adjust and adapt their business strategies to keep pace with the constant whims of the marketplace. This is a lesson E. Desmond Lee learned early in life. To remain competitive, a business must change with the times.

And the times were changing as Edgar Lee ascended to the presidency of Christian College. World War I had ended, giving way to the Roaring Twenties. Americans craved excitement. Editors of *The Fabulous Center, 1920-1930* (Time-Life Books) recorded:

"Almost anything, no matter how trivial or preposterous, seemed to give it to them – a gory murder in the tabloids, a world championship boxing match, a royal visit. In 1924, when Britain's young Prince of Wales made a pleasure jaunt to the United States, the nation went wild with excitement."

It was a time of flivvers, flagpole sitters and "flaming youth," of jazz and the birth of the "talkies" and radio, an age of prosperity. America was experiencing profound changes in morals. In particular, women were becoming liberated. They were casting their votes for the very first time. Despite the passage of prohibition, women were beginning to drink and to smoke.

Women's skirts were getting shorter too. As one newspaper article noted, "Women's hemlines are escalating so much lately that they are astonishingly nearer the knee than the ankle. Short is indeed the watchword for feminine apparel." Alarmingly, many demonstrated their new-found independence by competing with men. Divorce rates increased significantly. The rapidly changing relationships between the sexes engendered a conflict between social conservatives and modernists.

For the first time women were going to college in record numbers, and schools like Christian College were attractive Meccas for those whose parents preferred the semi-cloistered and closely monitored environment to the rowdiness and rebellion exploding on some co-ed campuses. Christian College was closely affiliated with the Disciples of Christ Church. The rules were rigid, strict and oppressive. The straight-laced, white glove and hat institution wasn't keeping pace with the changes going on in the outside world.

No Christian College girl could go to the Western Union Office, a doctor's office or even upstairs in any office building without a chaperone. None of the students could ride in an automobile without permission from the proper official or she would be subject to expulsion. This is where you begin to see Des' risk-taking personality.

"My first love was Kathleen Kelly, a student at Christian College whose mother was in charge of one of the dormitories. I was only 14, and she pointed out that I was too young for her daughter. But I frequently met Kathleen in the maintenance department to take her car-riding in my Ford flivver," Lee recalls. "Car-riding with a boy was a cardinal sin and usually led to expulsion. If we had ever been caught, it would really have embarrassed my father and he probably would have killed me."

Despite society's more progressive attitude toward women, many of the traditionalists on campus and in the community clung to the old ways of doing things. Edgar Lee's liberal viewpoint shocked and angered the traditional mindset.

But as a leader, Edgar Lee recognized the college must change in order to survive. So he greatly liberalized the rules and regulations for the young female students. He made it possible for Christian College girls to go downtown alone to a store, restaurant or beauty shop as long as it was on an approved list. Additionally, they were allowed to go to a "picture show" on a weekday afternoon and to a Saturday night movie if they had written permission from home.

In addition to relaxing the strict rules for the students, Lee remembers his father pushing for academic excellence at the college as well as a more democratic structure where the students would be held more responsible for their actions. Edgar Lee believed in the ability of the students to act as responsible citizens in the "college community."[1]

In an address to students, alumnae, faculty and friends on the schools' 142nd birthday, Des recalled his father introducing "a new system of student government where elections were democratic, and the students made the rules and decided on punishments for infringements."

"My dad involved women in all types of organizations. Scholars as well as college queens became campus leaders, and even a shy girl could find herself entering into activities and developing a sense of community service," he added.

As Allan Lemmon Hale notes in *Petticoat Pioneer, the Story of Christian College*, "It took courage to let fresh air into this atmosphere, but the new president was determined to do it immediately."

"My father hated the politics one always finds in a situation like that. You have to be an administrator and a leader. You have to inspire the students, be a person of integrity and a role model," Des reminisces.

COURAGEOUS LEADERS CONFRONT REALITY AND TAKE APPROPRIATE MEASURES

Leaders have an innate ability to size up the reality of any given circumstance. They have the skill to analyze situations objectively, in present terms – not what it used to be or what they would like it to be. While Edgar Lee had struggled tirelessly to redefine Christian College, he was a man of great integrity and knew when it was time to let go of the reins.

When Edgar Lee took over the presidency of Christian College, he inherited a debt of $135,000.[2] During the Twenties, he reduced that amount significantly but the stock market crash in 1929 eliminated any sense of security for the fledgling college. Seventy-one of the potential 310 students canceled in the fall of 1929. Budgets and salaries were dramatically cut.

During the ensuing years of the Depression, conditions continued in a downward spiral and war loomed on the horizon. By the end of 1934, as the United States reported 10.8 million unemployed and Hitler boasted the Reich would survive for one thousand years, President Lee recognized that he must step aside. He was a visionary – as his son would become. He was also a realist and he knew it was time to transition to new leadership.

"The board listened in silence as he gave his financial report for the fall semester," quotes author Hale. "They both knew it was the end. Another man might have gone into the next room and blown out his brains. Lee faced his trustees with courage."

"Gentlemen, I have done the best I could. I've worked hard. I've been honest. But in the face of times like these, my best has not been good enough." [3]

"During the Depression my dad would go to the small Missouri towns to try to interest the girls to come to Christian College," Des explains. "He did everything he could to keep the school going. He was not a merchandiser or a marketer, but he was a man of integrity and a man who believed in high standards of education. He was also a man who beat all kinds of odds. He came from a family with no resources and worked hard to accomplish something in his lifetime."

Like most great leaders, Edgar Lee had the ability to take an unbiased look at his own shortcomings as well as those of the organization. As another great Missourian President Harry S Truman once said, "The buck stops here," Edgar Lee did not point fingers and place blame – the responsibility rested with him. It would have been easy to blame the economy as many of today's business leaders and politicians often do. Instead, with dignity and courage he took responsibility for the college's state of affairs and stepped aside to make way, once again, for change.

In gratitude for his efforts, the trustees of the college named Edgar Lee "President for Life."

LEADERS OVERCOME PERSONAL CHALLENGES

"You can't have anything worthwhile without difficulties."

– Harry Truman

"In a way he was like the country he lived in, things came too easily." So wrote Robert Redford's character Hubell Gardner in the classic movie "The Way We Were." The line sums up the way we often look at our leaders. They are the lucky few, the chosen few, who appear to have talents and abilities which far exceed average folks. Seemingly, they live charmed lives where things come naturally and easily. Yet, many of today's business leaders have overcome enormous personal challenges. When you look back over their childhoods, you wonder how they pulled through. For example, Charles Schwab, who founded one of the largest discount brokerage houses, failed remedial English and nearly flunked out of college because he was dyslexic. Perhaps, these difficult personal experiences added to their characters an element of compassion and empathy – important leadership characteristics.

Throughout his life E. Desmond Lee has experienced personal challenges. While his father was working to build the fledgling Christian College in the 1920s, Des was growing into a young man and struggling with his identity. Outwardly, the young boy seemed happy-go-lucky, but inside he was plagued with self-doubt.

"I have struggled with myself all my life," he says. "I have felt insecure. I always wanted to do better than I was able to do." His desire to achieve, as with many successful people, often caused him to set nearly unrealistic expectations for himself.

"My insecurity, I think, is what has driven me. It was part of my makeup. But drive is another name for being determined to accomplish something. I have always felt as though I should have accomplished more than I have. People say I am hard on myself," Des adds.

At an age when most children are wondering what they will get for the holidays, Des was wondering and worrying about his future.

Both of Des' parents were academically accomplished. His mother was a Phi Beta Kappa and his father was given an honorary Phi Beta Kappa key because of his position and his grades at the University of Missouri. Education for the Lee children was a high priority, and the couple tried to instill a love of learning. Unfortunately, Desi – as his close friends often call him – was having difficulty in school.

"I couldn't get motivated. I felt my family was disappointed in me. I wasn't lazy, but I didn't get any stimulation from school. I was being accused of being slow," he explained. In fact, he often amuses his audiences today by telling them he flunked kindergarten.

"People think it's a joke when I say that, but I actually did. My father had the psychology department at the University of Missouri take a look at me and see if they could find out what was wrong with me because I wasn't motivated," he explains. "I finally kicked into gear but everyone agreed I should repeat kindergarten."

"One morning in the third grade, I remember going to the barn where I kept my bicycle. I had done poorly in school. But as young as I was, something turned on at that time, and I told myself I was going to have to change my life or I would be a total failure. That's when I turned my life around," Des explains.

After the revelation that day in the barn, Des went back to school and began to apply himself. "I said 'I am going to do the very best I can. I will listen to what the teacher says instead of sitting on my butt and doing nothing.'"

Grade school chum Charlie Digges remembers his classmate. "He was an outstanding person in grade school, always a good student. He always had a special smile, but also a prankish grin. He was up to playing jokes on people."

Today, Des is still known for his joshing, and he candidly admits some of it may be a defensive tool to camouflage his insecurity.

Des became quite popular, a young man with lots of friends, even though they teased him because of his height and big feet. (He towers over most at 6 feet, 4 inches.) He accepted the teasing good naturedly, but was known for turning the tables. Des was a real prankster – something he never outgrew.

"I remember once emptying all the bottles in the chemistry lab on the college campus. It is a wonder I didn't blow the place up," he says.

But just as things were looking up, Lee was transferred from the university school to a public school so he could participate in sports. Once again, he faced personal failure. But he learned from the experience the importance of not giving up.

"I tried out for the basketball team at Jefferson Junior High School, but coach Pug Fickland, turned me down. I was crushed. So my father talked to him and told him the reason I was at the school was because of the sports program and that it was a big disappointment that I hadn't made the team," Des explains.

Pug agreed to take another look and Des finally made the team. In his senior year he was named co-captain along with his boyhood friend Clay Cooper. "Our team beat everyone in the state. It shows how important parents can be in your development," Des notes.

LEADERS HAVE A COMPETITIVE SPIRIT

"We were all jocks of sorts. I mean, we played ball countless hours, played street hockey all night. That was everything. Sports were everything."
– Jack Welch, former CEO of GE

Sports were and still are an important element of Des Lee's life. He candidly admits he prefers athletics to academics – his happiest hours being spent shooting baskets. He also lettered in football, track, the discus and shot-put.

Even today, Des is perhaps one of the most competitive athletes for his age. Golf has replaced tennis and basketball as his favorite sport, and he is as determined to win on the links as he was on the basketball court. Although he knows he will never be another Jack Nicklaus or Arnie Palmer, his competitive spirit spurs him to spend many a sweltering day working with a pro, trying to improve his swing and lower his score to equal his age, now well into his eighties.

"I work on golf terribly hard now, the golf swing. I have learned a lot about the golf swing. I had a low handicap one time, and it went to hell. None of my friends are willing to work this hard but I'm not ready to give up," he explains.

Then he jokingly adds, "Tiger Woods works hard at his game and he has innate skills. Of course, he's more flexible than I am."

"Being competitive has always characterized my life. I don't want to be ruthless, but I want to be competitive. I want to accomplish things and, in the process, I want to be in the world. To accomplish things in the world you have to be a competitive person. But I have to draw that line between being ruthless and self-centered and self-serving and having the determination, perseverance and leadership qualities to build something worthwhile and allow others to join in," Des explains.

From a business perspective, Des notes that he learned four important lessons from participating in athletics throughout his life: Sportsmanship, companionship, competition and teamwork. As for sportsmanship, he says it is as important in life as it is in business to learn how to lose as well as win.

"Companionship is important because you've got to make life-long friends and never forget them," he explains. Friends are extremely important to Des and almost everyone who meets him becomes one of Des' friends because of his uncanny ability to really connect with people at all levels and from all walks of life. He has remained close to many of this childhood friends.

"In school, Desmond had time for everyone. Everyone teased him but they enjoyed him. They loved him. He was a very popular guy," says Clay Cooper, one of Des' teammates in high school.

"Desmond was an extrovert," says Earl Procter, another childhood friend. "We recognized his leadership qualities way back then."

Of course, no one can survive in the business world without being competitive. Des stresses the importance of winning, but he notes, "It's not about winning at all costs.

"One night after losing a basketball game, I was so mad I pounded on my locker and hit the door with my right arm causing a tremendous gash that took several months to heal because of an infection," he said. This was an important lesson for Des – not only to have determination and a desire to win, but to keep his temper and be a gracious loser.

Before teamwork became a management buzz word, Des embraced the concept in his business model. "The only way you are going to get the most out of employees is to make them feel they are a part of the team and that their contributions are important to the success of the venture. When you hire people, you begin by assessing the team's needs and then you hire people with diverse talents and encourage them to work together. You must understand that everyone is different, and we hired different types of people. No question about it," he says.

Call it a twist of fate, but athletics added another important dimension to Des' life – his friendship with classmate Sam Walton, the founder of Wal-Mart. Walton and Des were friendly competitors in their youth. They were both star athletes and leaders in school organizations. In a contest for student body president, Walton prevailed over Des.

"I always did say that when they elected him over me, they made the right choice," Des said. "He was my good friend, a wonderful guy, but ruthlessly competitive in everything he did – football, basketball and, ultimately, business. He was a better football player than I was, but I was a better basketball player."

Their lives continued to run parallel paths after they left high school as both built successful businesses and remained good friends. Des' company eventually became one of Wal-Mart's suppliers. "You can't make any money selling to Wal-Mart," Des notes with a smile and a warm chuckle.

"I remember Sam Walton appeared at one of our high school reunions. He and Des got to jawing and Des said, 'Sam, if you don't buy more of my stuff, I'm going to sell everything to Kmart.' He was a great admirer of Sam and said he got a lot of his ideas from Sam," says Clay Cooper.

"I learned a lot from Sam Walton and I have a lot of respect for him," Des explained. "He was my mentor. He destroyed a lot of Mom and Pop stores, but I'll tell you why. It's the inevitable result of science and business growth and size, which gives power to those who accumulate enormous resources.

"Although he was a ruthless competitor, he was wonderful with people. He would go to a store opening and go around and talk to all the people. When he'd speak he'd talk about his employees, and I learned from watching his people skills. He really had two personalities. While he was genuine and sincere with his employees, he used his power to make more money and expand his corporation. He had ruthless determination to build the business and he had people skills. That's the key to American business. I don't think they teach you that stuff in the Harvard MBA program," Des explains. "Sam symbolizes the American Dream. He never lost track of who he was. Sam was always Sam."

LEADERS RECOGNIZE PERSONAL STRENGTHS AND WEAKNESSES

Everyone has unique talents and special gifts. Unfortunately, nearly two-thirds of us don't realize our own personal strengths. We spend an inordinate amount of time focusing on our weaknesses and trying to improve those areas while ignoring the aspects of our life where we could excel. People who evolve into leaders have a clear understanding of their personal strengths, and they know how to utilize those things to achieve their goals.

While Des excelled at sports, he lacked musical talent. His mother was a gifted pianist. She had the ability to listen to a composition and immediately play it from memory. She hoped her son would also be a musician, but Des hated the piano and refused to practice.

"The only piano piece I ever learned to play with both hands was, 'Come with Me To See What Is in the Nest', Des notes.

In lieu of the piano and not being one to give up completely, Des took up playing the drums. He used his enthusiasm and charm to win a spot in the college orchestra, although at the time he was much younger than any of the other musicians.

"I was the youngest drummer in the state of Missouri. Now I think I'm the oldest," he jokes.

Always the entrepreneur at heart and wanting to help his financially struggling family, he started playing the drums at various gigs. "When I was in high school, I made extra spending money playing for dances out at the country club, but sometimes it was tough to see my friends dancing while I was up there on the bandstand."

Des also enjoyed working with his hands. He often spent time tagging along with Christian College maintenance supervisor Maurice Wightman. He eagerly offered to help do whatever needed to be done to keep the grounds and the buildings in good repair.

"I learned plumbing and pouring concrete, painting and rebuilding screens and windows. I also rehabbed dorm rooms, repaired furniture, dug ditches, and, I am sure, mowed the lawn at least 100 thousand times," he says.

Becoming a quite capable handyman, Des began to earn a salary. He started at ten cents an hour and worked up to twenty-five cents. "He was a tremendous craftsman," recalled Clay Cooper. "He was tenacious. He would be in the shop working on something and I would try to get him to go play basketball, and he wouldn't until he was finished with what he was doing."

"I loved to make things, such as toy boats and planes and model airplanes," Des said. "I was always trying to set up something, make something work, create something. There's no question about it, this experience helped me learn things that I used later in inventing things for my company."

Originally Des studied to be an engineer while attending Washington University. "I started out in engineering, but I realized from the very beginning that I didn't like the engineering courses because they were very mathematical and that wasn't my strong suit," he explains.

The dean of the engineering school suggested Des forget about an engineering degree because of its mathematical orientation. Instead, he counseled him to pursue business because of his great people skills.

"This was one of the best decisions of my life," says Des. Des worked as his company's first toolmaker and remained highly involved in the automation of the manufacturing process throughout his career.

[1] Columbia College, 150 Years of Courage commitment and Change, Paulina A. Batterson, page 101
[2] Ibid
[3] Ibid, 118

Des Lee, Missouri's youngest drummer

Des Lee and Team Members at Jefferson
Junior High School in Columbia, Missouri

Benetta Lee, Edgar Lee, Des Lee and
Virginia Lee

Edgar D. Lee, Des Lee's Father

CHAPTER TWO

LEADERS TAKE RISKS

"It was the best of times, it was the worst of times."
– Charles Dickens, A Tale of Two Cities

LEADERS TAKE RESPONSIBILITY FOR THEIR OWN SUCCESS

In the midst of the Great Depression and having resigned his post as president of Christian College, Edgar Lee moved his family from provincial Columbia, Missouri, where he had served as president of Christian College for 17 years, to University City – a suburb of Saint Louis. It was a solid, middle class area with a population of about thirty-two thousand. Neighborhood residents placed a strong emphasis on education – a comfortable fit for the Lees. To emphasize this civic quality, University City's founder had named the principal streets for outstanding schools such as Amherst, Princeton and Yale.

The heart of University City was the "Loop," which was where the streetcars made their turnarounds. It was also a retail shopping district. If you were among the fortunate few who had discretionary funds, you could buy fashionable clothes, groceries, automobiles and your children's favorite toys.

But this was the depth of the Depression and University City businesses, like businesses all across the country, were struggling. From 1929-1932 there were 85 thousand business failures in the United States. Street corners were populated with apple peddlers as bread lines and soup kitchens sprang up in nearly every neighborhood.

Times were hard as millions of Americans found themselves unemployed. The number of jobless ranged as high as 13 million – one worker in four. Newspaper headlines read: "U.S. Steel lays off another 10 thousand;" "Kentucky coal miners found living on dandelions;" and "110 children in New York City die from malnutrition." Of those who had jobs, most were receiving only subsistence wages. The annual per capita income in

1932 was only $495. If you had a job as a public school teacher, you might earn $1,200 a year, or as a waitress, $520 a year. Some restaurants advertised three large pork chops for thirty cents, roast beef for twenty cents and a vegetable dinner for a dime. A department store would sell you a sweater for $1.69 or a silk necktie for fifty cents.

Des remembers the story of one of his friends whose family had to take in boarders because her father's salary was cut drastically. "She would drive her mother to the market, and they'd purchase enough groceries for 16 people for a week for about five dollars." Of course, being able to buy groceries at all was good fortune. Many families were unable to put food on the table or shelter over their heads.

Banks were failing by the hundreds, and mills and factories were shut down. With no work available, many people could not pay their rent or their mortgages, and they were kicked out of their homes. Forced to seek alternative shelter, Hoovervilles – named after President Hoover, who was blamed for the conditions that led up to the Depression – sprang up across the country. These shantytowns were a collection of ramshackle tents and hovels – dismal and desperate conditions for thousands of people.

As one historian put it, "The great knife of the Depression had cut down impartially through the whole population, cleaving open lives and hopes of rich as well as poor. The experience had been more nearly universal than any prolonged recent emotional experience in [American] history."[4]

As a result, in the 1932 presidential campaign, Franklin D. Roosevelt had little difficulty in persuading voters that the only hope of recovery from the Depression lay in a change of administration. Winning by a popular vote of 57.4 percent, Roosevelt carried all but six states with 472 electoral votes to 59 for Hoover. With the country in a state of crisis, Roosevelt took the oath of office on March 4, 1933.

During the first one hundred days in office, Roosevelt went to work to create programs to give relief, create jobs and stimulate economic recovery for the U.S. economy. The plethora of public relief programs, often referred to as alphabet soup, breathed life and hope back into millions of American workers. Programs such as the Civilian Conservation Corps put 2.5 million unmarried men to work maintaining and restoring forests, beaches, and parks, and the Works Progress Administration provided work for 8 million Americans. The WPA projects included the construction or repair of schools, hospitals and airfields.

However, globally the Depression worsened and war-torn Germany was left vulnerable to the tyrannical propaganda of Adolf Hitler. The storm clouds of war began to loom over Europe.

While the world struggled, so did the Lee family. Fortunately, Edgar Lee found employment with the Equitable Life Assurance Society. From the few sales he was able to make, he valiantly tried to support his family. "I can remember how depressed he would be when he came home in the evening after a poor business day," says Des.

To make ends meet, the elder Lee taught American history at Jefferson College night school. Des watched as his father pondered over the test scores of his students to make sure he was being completely fair.

"My dad had many personal conferences with his students about their problems and their families since we were still in the Depression," Des explains. In his own business career, Des applied these same principles of fairness and concern when he evaluated his employees. Like his father, it was not a process he engaged in lightly.

While today many parents refuse to burden their children with their worries, the young people of the Depression-era were aware that money was scarce. The consensus was "we're all in this together," and they worked to make the best of the situation.

Never one to shy away from hard work, Des was eager to take whatever job he could get to earn money. During the summer months he worked on the Admiral excursion boat on the Mississippi River.

"I would go by bus and not get home until half past midnight, then I'd get up early the next morning to make the first voyage of the day. I ran the root beer stand on the dance floor. I remember the captain jumping on me when I was carrying a ladder through the crowd. He treated me like I was really dumb and he scared me to death," he says. "I decided I would never treat anyone who worked for me like that."

As difficult as these times were, it was a turning point in Des' life and a defining moment. Still a high school student, Des played defensive tackle and offensive end. He was also a track and basketball star. Although he was the new kid on the block, he had no problems fitting in. People liked him. He was elected class treasurer and later vice president. Under his picture in his high school yearbook there is a lengthy list of activities including the school opera and French club. Additionally, it was in this new environment that Des met his best friend and eventual business partner Jimmy Rowan.

Des leveraged his abilities as an athlete to win a basketball scholarship to Washington University. Utilizing his leadership skills, he eventually became the team's captain. He and Jimmy pledged Phi Delta Theta fraternity, and they both washed dishes and waited tables at the fraternity house to earn extra money. Additionally, he earned twelve dollars a month in a National Youth Administration job doing clerical work and cranking the mimeograph machine.

"I am a typical example of a C student who worked hard when I got into college," recalls Des. "I was elected to junior and senior honoraries, took part in extra-curricular activities and carried the load of two sports: track and basketball."

The senior honorary to which Des refers was, not surprisingly, for leadership, rather than academic scholarship. However, his athletic scholarship and the extra income he earned allowed him to take the most important step of his life.

LEADERS RECOGNIZE AND SEIZE OPPORTUNITY

"It was the worst investment anyone could possibly make. The chances of success were one in a million. We had few resources and every dime we had was important."
– E. Desmond Lee

A dream of independence and business enterprise was born in the heart of Desmond Lee on the campus of Christian College more than a half century ago. And as he struggled along in college with his modest jobs, his longing for financial success heightened. But in the Depression days, dreams were cheap. Making them come true was something else again.

"Jimmy and I used to talk all the time about going into business for ourselves when we got out of school. We even thought about going into the chicken business," Des explains.

With only fifty cents in their respective pockets, the two young men had no idea how they would finance even a small business enterprise, much less what the nature of the business would be. It seemed impossible.

Then, on a spring morning in 1939, destiny struck.

Des and Jimmy had hitched a ride to Washington University with Jimmy's father, John Rowan. On the back seat was a sturdy, odd-shaped piece of wire, roughly the contour of a trouser leg.

"What is that thing, Mr. Rowan?" Des asked.

For some reason, which at the time Des couldn't understand, the Rowans seemed reluctant to talk about it. But in the next two or three rides the persistent Des had his answer. It was a pants creaser – a popular washday aid in the days before permanent press fabrics were available.

"I had never even heard of a pants creaser," he recalled, "but I soon learned about it. A woman would have to stand over an ironing board for hours pressing the washed trousers that men wore. But with this invention, she could just slip a pants creaser into each leg of the trousers, hang them out to dry and the trousers would be creased."

John Rowan, an idea man and master salesman with a roller-coaster history of success and failure in a variety of businesses, had invented the pants hanger after a pair of his own trousers had fallen to the floor of his closet. The technology he used for his invention was so simple that he was able to make a sample out of a tin can with tin snips. He was having it manufactured in a Saint Louis shop and was selling it through Sears-Roebuck. The Sears buyer said the company would also be interested in a pants creaser, which the Saint Louis tool maker had invented and was manufacturing with crude tools in a basement.

"Mr. Rowan was told," Des remembers, "that if he succeeded in obtaining the patent for the pants creaser, he would never have to worry about income for the rest of his life."

Energized by the promise of wealth, Rowan located the inventor and was able to buy the patent for an adjustable fastener for the pants creaser and the inventor's tools for $1,500. Now Des understood all the secrecy. Rowan had hoped to form his own company, which would manufacture the pants creaser as well as the pants hanger. The problem was he didn't have the necessary start-up capital. Des and Jimmy, two young men scarcely out of their teens, saw their opportunity and jumped on it. They convinced Mr. Rowan to allow them to join in the business venture as partners.

Filled with enthusiasm and energy, Jimmy and Des discussed the embryonic venture until well past midnight. "We were just kids who wanted to do something. We wanted to accomplish something. We were both so poor, and we wanted an opportunity to work hard and make money."

"At two in the morning I rushed home and woke my parents and told them I wanted to go into business with the Rowans making pants creasers and pants hangers," Des said. "Dad thought I was crazy, and he told me to go to bed, and we'd talk about it in the morning. He was sure it was an impossible dream."

Certainly 1939 was no time to start a business. Many older and wiser businessmen would have warned Jimmy and Des to avoid such an endeavor. As Doris Kearns Goodwin wrote in No Ordinary Time, "No decline in American history had been so deep, so lasting, so far-reaching."

Edgar Lee, having experienced difficulties and disappointments at Christian College, tried to dissuade the young men. But they refused to listen. They were headstrong and armed with hope, youth, and optimism that prevented them from believing anything other than their dreams.

"Dad and Mr. Rowan didn't know each other, except through Jimmy's and my friendship. So we brought them together, and Mr. Rowan persuaded Dad that it was not an impossible dream at all, but a profitable business idea. Dad finally agreed to invest $2,500 he had saved for my education. I think he realized how much I wanted this. We found a few other investors, but I doubt if all of their monies added up to $10,000," Des said.

"It was the worst investment anyone could possibly make," he adds. "The chances for success were one in a million. We had few resources, and every dime we had was important."

And so with more daring than dollars, the four men organized the Lee/Rowan Company, manufacturing the pants hanger and pants creaser. Passion and desire fueled their efforts, and as they made their plans, they erased the word failure from their vocabulary. They had no choice now but to make the business a success.

The timing for launching a new business venture may have been bad, and so was the choice of location for the company's first offices. John Rowan found a home for the newborn company: A decrepit, four-story structure on Commercial Street, south of where the Gateway Arch stands in Saint Louis today. Once a lively commercial area for early Saint Louis factories and stores, the riverfront by the 1930s had become an ugly urban venue. The remnants of a Hooverville could still be seen, and homeless, jobless men huddled against the building to escape the winter cold or lay in the shade to escape the summer sun's blistering heat.

A few establishments remained open, but many of the surrounding, aged structures that covered the riverfront were now only red brick ghosts left behind as the city crept up the hill from the levee.

In the early 1930s, civic leaders had begun the years-long campaign to clear 40 blocks and, ultimately, to build the Gateway Arch as the centerpiece of the Jefferson Memorial. But roadblocks such as federal delays, citizen opposition and, later, the shadow of war, brought the project to a virtual standstill.

None of this mattered to Des and Jimmy, nor did it dampen their spirits. They saw their dream coming true. As George Orwell wrote: Ignorance is bliss.

"We knew that times were bad, but Jimmy and I were so excited about our new business that we didn't think much about the danger of going broke," explains Des.

For rent of $10 a month, the company occupied the first floor and half of the second. The first order of business was to clean the building, especially the one grimy, ill-equipped bathroom. Then the two good friends found old scarred desks and other furnishings stored on another floor, which they appropriated for their new business.

"We were right by the railroad tracks, and the windows were covered with soot. Jimmy and I tried to clean the windows. We worked all day, but we finally figured out that they were so stained by the trains that the more we scrubbed, the dirtier they seemed to get."

Manufacturing and merchandising their products were just as hard. They had to make their own tools or use ordinary home basement workshop tools. And there was very little capital to hire a labor force. The start-up workforce consisted of mostly poor people from the surrounding neighborhood. Although in those early days they made many mistakes, they persevered and slowly, day-by-day, they could see progress and could envision even more success.

"We made some initial sales with the pants creaser. Some of our first customers were Sears, Famous-Barr, J.C. Penny's and Woolworths. Our advertising slogan was 'Stop Ironing Wash Trousers; Save Work, Save Time, Save Money.' We ultimately sold them by the thousands to all the department stores all over the United States," Des remembers.

"We kept manufacturing the pants creasers for years. That's what built the company in the beginning. They had an automatic lock, which was one of the things I designed," Des says proudly.

The work was hard, but the dream of success was an elixir for aching muscles and lack of sleep. Like many true entrepreneurs, the journey of building from the ground up and the early struggles were some of the most exhilarating. As Jim Rowan noted, "Regardless of the task, we were eager to do the job. I look back on those days with all their frustrations, and I realize that they were some of the best years of my life."

Each of the company's founders brought his own expertise to the organization creating a strong team – a strategy that remained an integral part of Lee/Rowan's success. Mr. Rowan and Jimmy were the sales and marketing arm of the organization. Edgar Lee knew nothing about manufacturing or sales, but was gifted in working with people so he was in charge of production and personnel. Des was put in charge of the shop. "Our tools were pretty crude, but they worked, and eventually we designed a lot of machinery for manufacturing our products," Des explains. "Bringing different personalities together enabled us to work together."

In the early days, Jimmy Rowan quit college and worked for the company full-time, but Des' father refused to allow him to quit school so Des worked weekends and vacations until he completed his education.

"Jimmy played a major role and we enjoyed working together. We prided ourselves on becoming the best packers of pants creasers, seeing which one could pack more in less time in order to get them delivered to the customers sooner," Des reminisces.

Eventually, Des was offered a graduate scholarship to Harvard Business School, which he turned down. This prompted his sister to urge his father to shut the struggling business down and encourage Des to go to work for a large corporation. "Thank God I didn't do that," Des notes.

"Back then, you didn't hear much about MBA programs. I often wonder what difference that would have made in my life. Harvard people are some of the most successful big-time operators in the world. But there is an elite image, and that is not compatible with me. Plus, I felt I had to stay with Lee/Rowan to help it survive."

But it wasn't easy. With the weak economy and their slim capital, even the senior Rowan's marketing prowess wouldn't always succeed. They were too poor to hire delivery trucks so they made their early deliveries in their own automobiles.

"We would take our fathers' cars, load them up and drive up to the receiving docks of the stores. We'd take the out-of-town shipments to the post office."

Bookkeeping responsibilities were assigned to Des, but his performance was less than impressive. "I was the company's first and worst bookkeeper. I made a sixty-four-cent error that no one could ever reconcile," Des acknowledges.

A sixty-four-cent error may not sound like a lot, but at the time the company was teetering on the edge. Every penny counted. Early bank balances ranged from $12.63 in 1939 to $221.81 at the end of 1941. In those first few years, it was a slippery slope and the Lees and the Rowans easily could have slid into bankruptcy.

But the word failure was not part of their vocabulary. "What else could we have done?" asks Des. "We had no other place to go."

LEADERS STAND BEHIND THEIR PRODUCT

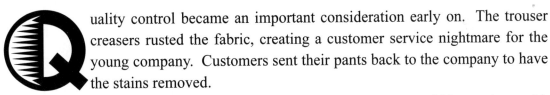uality control became an important consideration early on. The trouser creasers rusted the fabric, creating a customer service nightmare for the young company. Customers sent their pants back to the company to have the stains removed.

"My father, a Phi Beta Kappa and college president, spent most of his evenings with some sort of chemical we found that would take the rust out. Then he would send the trousers back to the customer who had returned them," Des explains.

Of course, the founders also recognized the need to remedy the rust problem. "At first, we experimented with having the wire plated in a local plating shop, but we had no control over how much plating they put on. We learned the best thing to do was to use galvanized wire."

Working out such production problems was Des' responsibility – a challenge he eagerly accepted because, since boyhood, he had loved to "make things and make them better."

There was also a problem with the pants hanger. "It turned out to be a lousy one," Des explains. "It went on the inside of the cuff, but it had sharp edges and it would tear the threads on the pants. We dropped it pretty quickly and made a better version of it years later using the same basic principle, but using plastic coating so it wouldn't hurt the trousers."

The seasonal nature of their primary product, the pants creasers, also presented a challenge. Pants creasers only sold in the summertime when washable trousers were worn. So the founders used their innovative talents – which would become the hallmark of the company – and developed a host of new products. They added a tie press, a thread and needle kit that was molded from plastic, a plastic hanger, a tie rack, sweater driers, glove driers, girdle driers, lingerie driers and sock driers. Gradually, the profit and loss statement transitioned from red to black.

"Even though we were still depending on simple and crude methods of manufacturing, we became the major drier firm in the country," Des said.

That doesn't mean they didn't make errors. "We made many mistakes," Des acknowledged. "We misjudged the market many times and had to make do with what we could afford."

As the numbers of products increased, so did the company's employee base. Within the first two years, the staff grew to 15, and they needed more space for their factory. They moved to a larger but equally decrepit building. It was an old, abandoned brewery that was in such bad shape that one day the first floor collapsed and a load of steel crashed through to the basement.

"We were making a lot of our own tools, and I used to go down into the basement to harden the tool steel in a blacksmith's forge. I might have been there when that steel fell. But I guess I just wasn't supposed to die that day," Des said.

Times were tough for the Lee/Rowan team, but there were reasons for optimism. Many were predicting the worse part of the Depression was over, and the economy was recovering. But another, perhaps even greater crisis loomed on the horizon – the onset of World War II.

Three Generations: Grandfather Lee, Des Lee, and Edgar Lee

Des Lee in Front of the Mediterranean Sea in Africa during World War II

CHAPTER THREE
SURVIVING THE WAR YEARS

Talk to Des Lee for any length of time and his love of his family, his friends, his community, his God and his country becomes clear. His love of country was founded during his gallant service in World War II. That service challenged his notions of equality, forged his courage, honed his understanding of suffering and enhanced his management and engineering skills. But the war also posed vast problems for the growing company, including pulling away its two young instigators at just the time their innovation and sweat equity were sorely needed.

****

America's entry into World War II created new economic challenges. The American people had to fight the battle of production for it was their task to produce the enormous quantities of munitions, clothing and food needed for the worldwide conflict. The war also meant the great dislocations of men, including Jimmy Rowan and Desmond Lee. The two fathers, Edgar Lee and John Rowan, were left behind to keep the company afloat through difficult years.

"Jimmy and I would not let our fathers give up," Des said. And the two men pledged to their sons they would not let the business go under in spite of wartime restrictions.

"The government had practically shut down our firm because no steel was available in wartime," explains Des. "So John Rowan went to the ordnance department and said the company couldn't survive without government contracts."

The government gave Lee/Rowan contracts for several products. It became a supplier of arming wires for the Army Air Corps and the Navy. An arming wire is a small wire with several attachments that runs down from the bombardier cockpit to arm the bombs.

"Lee/Rowan found an ingenious method to manufacture these arming wires, and the competition was using very complicated machines. So the ordinance department came to our little plant and required us to show our competitors, who were all much larger than we were, how to make them. We made millions of them. That's what kept the company going. In fact, Lee/Rowan became one of the outstanding defense firms during the war," Des notes.

In addition to arming wires, John Rowan and Edgar Lee buoyed the cash flow by selling Mexican jewelry to keep the firm afloat until Des and Jimmy returned.

THE BOYS IN UNIFORM

"This is no time for ease and comfort. It is time to dare and endure."
– Winston Churchill

At the tender age of 21, Des was inducted into the service as a private. His military career began at Fort Leonard Wood near Lebanon, Missouri, which is located in the central part of the state. After his indoctrination, he was retained as a cadet to train other soldiers. Subsequently, he was accepted for officer candidate school in Fort Belvoir, Virginia.

"The Officers' Candidate Training School was the most vigorous program I had ever experienced from both a mental and physical standpoint," Des remembers. So strenuous, in fact, that he almost washed out because he contracted spinal meningitis just at graduation time.

"I was so weak when I got out of the hospital I told the commanding officer I just couldn't finish out the final week of training. He told me I was out of the program, but then his superior officer reversed the decision, and they allowed me to graduate."

Faced with the reality of being shipped overseas, Des had some unfinished business to tend to. During college, he had dated Margery Stauffer, the sister of a fraternity brother.

The popular, athletic, sandy-haired co-ed and Des had dated during their senior year. Informally, they had discussed marriage, but Margery firmly explained she wanted to wait until he could be established in his career. However, circumstances had changed, and Des didn't want to wait any longer.

"I called her, and I told her I was going to go overseas. I proposed to her over the phone. She said she'd talk to her father and call me back," says Des.

The next day Margery did call back and her answer was "Yes." The two were married at the home of her parents, and their honeymoon was a train trip to Fort Bragg, North Carolina, where they set up housekeeping in a small home in nearby Fayetteville.

Des was assigned to command African-American troops, the 384th Engineers. Now keep in mind, Des grew up in a nearly all-white world that clung to the principle and practice of segregation. While he was never guilty of a strong racial prejudice – and certainly he inherited none from his parents – he was a creature of the times and accepted segregation as a way of life.

However, his command post was a life-changing experience for Des and ultimately had a profound impact on his leadership style. He was appalled by the gross prejudice and discrimination he observed. "I think when I worked with the black troops in World War II, I gained a new sense of compassion for minorities," he explained.

"This was my first exposure to the seriousness and tragedy of race relations, especially in small southern towns. An African-American soldier had no acceptance and was considered dirt and a target for extreme discrimination. I fought this battle the best I could since I became very attached to my troops.

"We had one situation in camp when a racist second lieutenant, a guy from West Point, was assigned to my company. He got upset with one of the men and fired a shot into the ground. I went to the commander of the battalion and told him to get the guy out of here before nightfall or we would have bloodshed. And he was out."

Commanding troops taught Des valuable managerial skills. "You have to learn to work with all kinds and all types of people. I remember once being on maneuvers, and we were told to build tents for all the officers for a special deal they were having. I created a production line. Everything went quickly and smoothly. The colonel said he didn't believe that it could be done like this. I used all the troops to do it like building an automobile, and I knew how to do that sort of thing."

As a result of his innovative approach to the project, Des was transferred to the engineering corps where he sharpened his skill as an engineer. But while the military taught him much about leadership, it also placed him in grave danger.

"Margery had been with me for only about two months before I was sent overseas." Des remembers. "I was stationed in Fort Dix, and Margery was planning to come for a visit from Fort Bragg when I got the orders we were shipping out. I had to call her and tell her not to come. I didn't get to see her before I left. I told her I loved her, and I hoped I would return."

Margery left Fort Bragg and returned to Saint Louis as Des began his journey across the ocean to North Africa. "Our ship crossed over several German submarines and we dropped depth bombs, which apparently destroyed them. It was a scary experience," says Des.

While stationed in North Africa, Des and his troops ran a box factory to make storage containers preparing for the invasion.

"The commanding general also wanted lawn chairs for his officers' club, so I designed the chairs and set up an assembly line for production. We were given three days to do the job. At the end of that time, we had 300 chairs," Des proudly explains.

At one point, after D-Day, Des was ordered to go south into a little town five miles away for reconnaissance. Alone, he started the journey, checking out bridges and roads in order to report their condition. As he continued his hike, people began to come out of their hiding areas to meet him.

"At first I was scared. Then, they started offering me their bicycles, and they told me how wonderful the Americans were. They also were delighted to be free, but they were still afraid of Germans in the area even though they had been liberated. Hundreds of people surrounded me and followed me for three or four miles as I made my way back to headquarters," Des remembered.

Des also volunteered as an engineer with the Army Air Corps and flew over the Siegfried Line. The Siegfried Line was built by the Germans to protect their border and was deemed to be nearly impenetrable.

"It was an Air Force bombing raid of 20 planes. I volunteered for interservice experience, not realizing how dangerous it was. The German anti-aircraft guns fired shells with shrapnel going in all directions. When I returned from that exercise, I found the plane I was in had 26 holes in it. I was a damned fool, but at that time I was fearless," he says.

Des was also stationed on the beach located near the town of Anzio, Italy. The Allied forces had taken Anzio beach with relative ease, but within the next week as the Allies prepared to push farther inland, the Germans gathered troops to eliminate what Adolf Hitler called the Anzio Abscess. During the next several months, some of the most savage fighting in World War II ensued.

"I was shot at many times. On Anzio beachhead, I heard a sniper's bullet and hid behind a rock until the shooting stopped. You were always afraid of being hit. Planes would fly over day and night. They would strike the beachhead during the day and would bomb us all night. You never knew where the bombs would hit. Fortunately, I was never wounded.

"Our headquarters at Anzio were in wine cellars where the wine was stored in huge barrels. It wasn't surprising that some of the guys got into the wine. But then that was one way of survival because the Germans were shelling us all the time.

"It took over two months for the Americans to start moving the enemy back. We were scared that we would be pushed right into the ocean. I really thought we were finished.

"As we moved out of Anzio, we were pinned down by gunfire in a small town. I tried to rescue one man who had been wounded when a whole truckload of ammunition was bombed, and shells were going off one by one. His leg had been blown off and he was dying. Unforunately, I couldn't save him," Des remembers.

Des was eventually promoted to captain and received the Silver Star for going behind the lines to retrieve a boat that had been left on a river. It was important not to allow the boat to fall into enemy hands.

"The colonel ordered me to get some other men and get that boat, and you don't argue with a colonel," recalls Des.

The group successfully pulled the boat out of the water and got it back on the truck. "The German troops had evacuated by then, but they were starting to come back. If the Germans had known we were there, we would have been machine-gunned."

After the war in Europe, Des was placed in charge of troop trains, including one train that ran over Brenner Pass. Brenner Pass is 59 miles long and 4,495 feet high. It connects Innsbrook, Austria, with Bolzano, Italy. Throughout its history it has been of strategic importance, but after Word War I, it became the border between Italy and Austria. During World War II, as the Allies pushed the German infantry north, the imposing Alps Mountains impeded enemy troops from reaching the safety of Austria. The only way to cross the Alps was through the Brenner Pass.

The pass was important to the Germans in another way. It was the route they used to funnel supplies down from Austria to ground troops in Italy. Because of that importance, it came as no surprise that the Germans kept the pass heavily armed with artillery at all times. Destroying enemy activity through Brenner Pass was a prime tactical target for the Allied Forces.

"Once I was taking some troops out and didn't see a break in the rail. The enemy was always dynamiting, and we were often in danger. At that time, we thought we were in trouble because the steam engine had turned over, and we all thought we'd be scalded to death. Somehow, I managed to escape," Des remembers.

"I witnessed tremendous death and destruction. One man lives and one man dies. I often said to myself, 'If I am fortunate enough to survive and return home, I want to do something worthwhile with my life.'"

While Des was fighting on the European front, his chum and business partner, Jim Rowan was a naval officer in the Pacific and was facing many of the same dangers. Both Des and Jim had gone into service with a boyish idealism and staunch patriotism. The idealism may have tempered a bit with the years, but the patriotism has never faded.

"We thought we were fighting a war for democracy and preservation of the principles and ideals on which this nation was founded. We were fighting against the evil Nazi leaders who were trying to dominate the world and willing to destroy human life in torture chambers to further their cause. This idealism brought us all together. The idealism and tragedy motivated us to continue the battle.

"It was the time of Rosie the Riveter, of the men and women who went into factories for supplementary income, and to support the service people overseas. I was glad to be part of it.

"Today, it would be very hard to sell that concept because we are better informed about the economics and politics of the world and the fact that wars are a doubtful way of solving man's problems.

"Relatively speaking, we were more naïve 50 years ago compared to what we are today. Most Americans don't believe in becoming involved in any major conflict. It's hard enough to get them excited to protect the values that are worthwhile," Des comments.

THE BOYS COME HOME –
MATURING INTO MANAGERS

By 1945, World War II was over and in a few months Des and Jimmy were in Saint Louis, designing and manufacturing pants creasers, pants hangers and driers of all kinds.

Matured in their war experiences, Des and Jim may not have been the blithe spirits who had helped start the company six years earlier, but they hadn't lost their enthusiasm. They still believed strongly in their dreams and were as committed as ever to turning their business into a successful enterprise.

Lee/Rowan's war profits from government contracts were used to finance a new plant. But even in the new surroundings, the furnishings were modest to say the least – amounting to nothing more than a hodge-podge of used furniture. And business practices were equally unsophisticated. So when approached to buy into a national advertising campaign the young entrepreneurs were unequipped to assess the value of such an investment. Eager to build their business endeavor, they dreamed of the big time with their heads in the clouds.

"The head of an advertising agency came to us with the idea that we would have an artist create an advertisement showing a Lee/Rowan girl hanging a pair of trousers on the clothes line to advertise the pants creaser. It was a full page in color and was to run in Better Homes and Gardens, movie magazines, Good Housekeeping and Life. It would cost us about $200,000."

At the time of this deliberation, Lee/Rowan's revenues amounted to no more than 300 thousand dollars. Nonetheless, the decision was made to undertake the national campaign. The result – the ad campaign was a huge bust.

"We had three inquiries, and we didn't sell a single item," Des says. "We were strapped financially. We were out of cash to pay our employees. Plus, there were other unpaid bills and the installments on the advertising campaign. One day, John Rowan went into my father's office and said, 'Well, Edgar, I think we are broke.'"

The glamorous advertising campaign nearly forced the company into bankruptcy. But that didn't break their spirits. Despite financial troubles nothing was going to stand in the way of their dreams.

As with most leaders, Des used this episode as a learning experience. "Never undertake a national advertising campaign unless you have the resources to finance it," Des cautions. "We learned that the best way was to advertise in the local newspaper where people do business with the local stores."

Returning to an area of the business he knew best, Des started designing new products back in the tool room. "I was in charge of the tool room, once again building the tools used to make products."

To enhance his skills, Des went back to Washington University in Saint Louis and took courses in electrical and mechanical engineering and tool design. But maintaining and growing the business was a constant struggle – always touch and go.

Des remembers that at one point as the company was growing, one of their competitors could have bought the entire net worth of the business out of petty cash. "Through perseverance, we eventually drove them out of business."

Not long after returning from the service, Jim Rowan became wistful for the West Coast. He had spent part of his military service there and had fallen in love with the ocean. For a while, he tried to put it out of his mind as he and Des worked to build Lee/Rowan, but the lure became stronger and stronger. Eventually, he told Des that while he would always be a part of Lee/Rowan, he wanted to create a life in California. Sadly, he said he had made the gut-wrenching decision to leave the company.

A disappointed but understanding Des accepted Jimmy's decision. Jim would retain an interest in the company, but most importantly, the two best friends made a pact that their friendship would never falter. "The early struggles together created a bond and will never be forgotten," Des explained.

With Jimmy's departure, Des had growing authority, but he remained respectful of the two elder partners.

Leaders Take Risks and Don't Fear Failure

Innovation was the mainstay of the Lee/Rowan philosophy long before management gurus began to preach about it like a religion. For example, one of the first products the company made after the pants creaser and pants hanger was a sock drier. Typically, sock driers had been made in every size, but Des had a better idea.

"I designed a tube with a rod that would adjust the length. I convinced Mr. Rowan that it would be a terrible mistake to have all these different frames made and shipped out. We should do something creative and different, and he agreed. We had adjustable sock driers in every department store. They sold like hot cakes. Plus, the new design kept the socks from shrinking so we were finding the answers to simple problems," Des explains.

Des refused to accept the status quo. The competitive spirit he embraced in athletics served him well in business. He had an insatiable desire to do things better. In a highly competitive environment that drive to be a step above the rest set Lee/Rowan apart from other companies.

According to Des, "The world is competitive. Everything we touch is competitive. That is what stimulates human beings to do the things they do. That is what drives the economy of the world."

Almost every day, Des would think up an idea for a new product, sit down at his desk and create a design. Sweater driers, girdle driers, glove driers, and tie racks. Long before the days of sophisticated market research, Des understood the importance of keeping pace with market trends. "We did not do scientific market research. We weren't trained to do that."

It's a good thing Des had a creative mind because with the invention of new fabrics and technological advances, the demand for the wire driers literally dried up. So the company realized it would have to switch directions if it was going to survive. Des had been known to say that innovation keeps everyone's interest alive. It keeps the company and its people vibrant and involved.

In order for Des and the others to design more products, the company needed an operations person who could wear many hats. Robert Luerding came on board in the late forties to fill that position. Other management positions were added including Russ Zang as secretary/treasurer and John Moritz to purchase raw materials.

"We went into all kinds of things to try to make a living. We made beer-taper stands and any kind of work we could get in order to survive," explains Des.

A 24-carat gold-plating facility was added for the company to gold-plate everything from towel racks to clothes hangers. "We used gold-plate over nickel, and the products were beautiful. I wound up gold-plating a lot of putters for my golf buddies. The problem was no one believed that it was real gold."

Keeping up with the times, the company entered the closet accessory business with skirt racks, blouse racks, garment racks and a variety of hangers. The hangers were so popular that Lee/Rowan received an order from one of the British royal family. "One of the things that made us grow so big was the Add-a-Hanger where one hanger could be hung from another to save space. One of the tool makers and I developed the idea. It has been copied all over the world," Des explains.

The 1950s ushered in rock 'n' roll along with the Lee/Rowan Roll-Away Slacks Carrier and the Roll-Away Skirt Carrier. Both were advertised as a handy way to hang eight slacks or skirts. "Great for hanging fresh ironing, too," Des added. The retail cost: $4.56 for the slacks hanger and $5.13 for the skirt hanger. Other products included: the Cuff-Master pants hanger, $7.20 per dozen; Skirt Add-A-Hangers, $6.75 per dozen; Drip-Dry Hanger, $7.20 per dozen; and the Blouse Tree, $6.25 per dozen.

A 1955 price and information sheet offered a Knee-Hi Sock Dryer that retailed for $1.50 a pair; a Marvel Sock Dryer, for $1.25 a pair; the Deluxe Lingerie Dryer for $1.98 each; and the Tru-Fit Sweater Dryer for $2.49 each (adult size). Then as panty hose became popular, there was the vinyl covered, rust-proof, run-proof, snag-proof, panty hose dryer.

Design was so much a part of Des that it rarely left his mind. One day, Mr. Rowan thought he had suffered a heart attack, so Des took him to the doctor's office. "As I sat in the lobby waiting for him, I designed a tie rack. That rack has been used all over the world. I use mine daily in my own home," Des says.

As the company grew in the number of product offerings, additional space was needed.

In 1964, an second plant was opened in Jackson, Missouri, about two hours south of Saint Louis.

"Being a leader in any industry means constantly innovating changes and upgrading manufacturing, distribution, delivery and promotion of a product,"
— Gary Lee, Des' son and former CEO of Lee/Rowan

Most of the company's product introductions were successful, but not all.

Some were total failures, and those Des discarded as lessons learned.

"We made a lot of products that we buried, and we did that until the very end. A doggy cot failed. We had a pedal gym exerciser, but we were way ahead of our time and that was a complete failure," Des explains.

"Many of the early products went down the drain, but we were able to shift with the market demand. When something failed, we always tried to come back with a new idea. That was a secret of our success.

"We had to keep an open mind, to listen, to be willing to cast aside those things that failed and give our energies to those things that succeeded."

One of the biggest failures the company endured was its foray into the toy manufacturing business. In 1968, Des acquired Modern Crafts Company of Saint Louis. The company primarily manufactured toys and children's related furniture. Initially, Des saw the acquisition as an opportunity to diversify – not only in terms of product, but also in materials. By this time, Lee/Rowan had become a bathroom and closet accessories manufacturer and almost exclusively used wire and steel tubing in its manufacturing process. Modern Crafts utilized wood and wood products. Until the buyout, some of the upholstery and woodworking on the Lee/Rowan products had to be provided by outside suppliers. But with the addition of the toy company, that could now be handled in-house.

Unfortunately, the advantages brought by diversification did not outweigh other factors unique to the toy industry that Des had failed to evaluate in the overall analysis.

"I thought I'd make something big out of the toy business. Then, I realized I couldn't finance the thing.

"In the toy business May, June and July were the selling months, but you didn't get paid until December because the retailers didn't sell until then. As a small company, we had to pay for raw materials in February and March. A couple of retailers went bankrupt on us. It was obvious we weren't making any money. We were in products that weren't going to grow, and there was no profit margin in it. I almost wrecked the company."

After ten years in the toy manufacturing business, Des sold it.

"That's the penalty you pay for innovation, and it's very expensive. But it's true no matter what the size of your business. It's true for General Electric, Southwestern Bell and General Motors. When you innovate and try to do something different, you take a chance on failing. But you have to have the guts to do that. That inner feeling that no matter what happens, you are going to try," Des explains.

"What industry is looking for today is for people willing to take a risk. In our nation, there is great opportunity for people willing to take a risk, to be innovators and develop new things. Doing this is not always good. Many things will fail, but risk taking is the process which allows the individual and nation to grow."

As President Harry S. Truman once said, "No one who accomplished things could expect to avoid mistakes. Only those who did nothing made no mistakes."

Sagely, Des advises, "Don't be afraid of failure. Take risks as long as you are able."

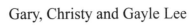
Gary, Christy and Gayle Lee

Margery and Des Lee

Des Lee in Africa, 1942

Jackson, Missouri Groundbreaking Ceremony, 1969

CHAPTER FOUR

LEADING INTO A NEW ERA

LEADERS STEP BOLDLY INTO THE FUTURE

As the world was introduced to color television, Elizabeth II was crowned queen of England, John Kennedy married Jacqueline Bouvier, Rocky Marciano retired undefeated, Elvis joined the Army, and the Hula-Hoop made it big – Lee/Rowan turned the corner and was beating out its competitors. A new plant that had been financed with profits from government contracts during the war had been expanded, and the burgeoning company now employed nearly 200.

Innovation and diversity continued to be the key to growth. Trade shows served as an incubator of ideas for the innovative Des. He reminisces about going to every industry show imaginable from premium items to plumbing fixtures.

"We would go to shows in Chicago and New York and look at all the displays. If we thought a product might fit into our merchandise mix, we would copy it and adapt it with enough changes that we wouldn't be stealing the patent. We always tried to make things better," Des notes.

Creative thinking was the key according to Des. He would wake up in the middle of the night and have an idea. Then he would spend time with the designer developing the idea after everybody else went home.

By the mid-'70s, Des' commitment to diversification and innovation was paying off. He wrote to his employees, "I am happy to report to you that we are looking forward to the biggest year in our history in the midst of pessimism, increasing unemployment, worldwide inflation and the energy crisis. Our company has passed through several years of poor business, but we are emerging stronger than ever, and at a time when many companies are cutting back, we are forging ahead in sales," he said.

Unfortunately, the company might have been forging ahead, but Des' personal life was taking a tragic downturn. In January 1977, his beloved wife Margery was diagnosed with cancer. She passed away nine months later at the age of 56.

Margery was Des' pillar of strength as he diligently and passionately worked to build Lee/Rowan. She encouraged him when times looked bleak and celebrated with him when there were successes. Although she originally thought she couldn't have children, she had given him three wonderful children – Gary, Christy and Gayle. She had also taken a leadership role in the community, involving herself in numerous projects. And now the vivacious co-ed Des had fallen so madly in love with more than 35 years ago was gone.

"I was devastated. It was a very hard blow," Des says. "However, we talked a lot during that last year, and even though the circumstances were bad, it was a happy time for us. I think you get beyond all the trivial things you get bogged down in, and you are more tolerant."

"Just before Margery passed away, the family gathered around her bed, and she told us, 'Nothing in the world is worth more than love. It is the only worthwhile thing.' Her words have remained with me to this day," Des states.

A New Chapter

After Margery's death, Des continued to pour his energies into Lee/Rowan, but his life was somewhat empty without his wife. Then, he met Mary Ann Taylor. Actually, he had known Mary Ann because her former husband was a friend and the founder of Enterprise Leasing – another well-known Saint Louis company. In 1979, Mary Ann became Des' wife.

"I am very fortunate to have had two wonderful women in my life. Mary Ann is a tremendous person," notes Des.

As he began a new chapter of his personal life, Des faced new challenges in his business life too. As the company stepped into the 1980s, the country was in the height of a recession. Interest rates soared over 21 percent, which created a serious problem for Lee/Rowan. The company borrowed funds to purchase the raw materials to produce inventory. This situation was complicated by the fact that sales had been seriously curtailed. Strict cost control measures were put into place throughout the company, and the engineering department had to respond quickly to find less expensive ways to produce products. Plastic hangers were added to the wood and wire hanger line.

The next step was the shelving business. Des, who refused to fear failure, called Gary Lee and Charlie Lammers, who at the time was vice-president of Modern Crafts Toy Division, into his office and asked them, "Do you know anything about shelving?" They shook their heads no, and he said, "Well, you better start learning because I just bought a wire shelving company."

Actually, Des had bought two small companies to start the shelving, storage and organizational division. He utilized Lee/Rowan's extremely crude equipment as the base for this new venture. The first machine made one four-foot length of shelving at a time. Des also purchased some machines from another small company and used them until he could afford more sophisticated and powerful equipment.

This new venture turned out to be a good move and quickly became the company's fastest growing segment. The Builder's Division, headed by Charlie Lammers was a financial turnaround for the company. The product mix included ventilated metal shelving, closet organizers, garage organizers and other wire and tubing products, which were epoxy-coated. In fact, Lee/Rowan became one of the largest epoxy-coating operations in the country with four automated lines.

The equipment used to manufacture the shelving was specially designed and built in the U.S. and Switzerland. Des himself had a lot of input into the development of these sophisticated machines. Productivity was high as these machines could make 27 miles of shelving every 24 hours.

"Our greatest growth came in the shelving business, because it was a product everyone needed in the home whether through the builder or home improvement store or discount center. It would appeal to the mass-market department stores, catalogs, variety stores, specialty stores, bath shops, mail order retailers, etc."

The company's goal was to have eight percent of annual sales come from new products. "We tried to be innovative in all phases of our business. Our goal was to 'do it better.'"

The company maintained a policy that the door is always open for new ideas. And the customers loved the results. Madeline Shea from Bronx, New York, wrote a note to thank the engineering department for the simple design of her garment rack. "It is exactly what I needed, and the price is so unbelievably reasonable."

The engineering department worked busily to introduce new products. An over-door shoe rack and an over-door shelf unit that could be "knocked down" for customer assembly was added in the mid-'80s. Also added to the mix was a floor-to-ceiling closet organizer with revolving shoe racks that could hold 12 pairs of shoes. Revolving tie racks, bath vanity benches, plastic tie racks and belt racks to snap over wire-formed structures were included in the line.

In 1992, under the direction of Des' son, Gary, the company introduced an interactive kiosk "that walked a consumer through a variety of storage options. It provided answers to consumers' specific questions so they could buy knowledgeably," said Kent Heltne, Lee/Rowan's general merchandise manager. "For the retailer, this means having a fully informed, non-salaried salesperson always available."

LEADERS THINK GLOBALLY

"Companies that don't adapt to changing markets are not going to make it. It's going to be one world and one market eventually."

– Des Lee

In 1990, Lee/Rowan's Retail Vice President Jim Morley attended the Frankfurt Fair, the world's largest international exposition meeting with sales agents, importers and retailers from the world market. Although ten other manufacturers had hangers on display in Frankfurt, Morley explained that many countries showed an interest in the company's high quality and innovative plastic hangers. The question became: "Is the company ready to expand to a world market?"

Des and his team didn't jump, but rather took a studied and cautious approach. "There were the obvious language differences, but there were strategic differences in marketing outside the U.S. as well. We wanted to make sure we understood the parameters," Des said.

In the U.S., Lee/Rowan was used to dealing with discounters, but in other countries the distribution network consisted primarily of department stores, home centers, hyper-markets and small specialty stores. Lifestyle issues presented another challenge. Homes throughout the world vary greatly in size and construction. Most do not have walk-in closets, and some have no closets at all. For the manufacturer of closet organizing systems, this posed a problem. Nonetheless, some of the products were universal in design such as free-standing baskets, shoe racks, garment racks and shelving.

The potential was there for Lee/Rowan to become an international entity – to expand onto the worldwide stage. "The world lives in smaller quarters than we, yet there is no worldwide product on the market," Morley said. "The remedy is Lee/Rowan…where the world gets organized."

That became the company's new tag line, and the foray into the international business evolved into an integral part of the business operations – eventually accounting for about five percent of the total mix. With the addition in November 1990 of an international sales representative, Kees Van Straalen, Lee/Rowan's sales extended to Europe, Japan, the Far East, Mexico, Australia, New Zealand and Canada.

"To sell internationally, you have to begin by selling the company," Van Straalen noted. "When you are selling overseas, you have to cultivate a relationship, nurture it, and then make your sales."

Additionally, in 1990 Lee/Rowan began to import products from Taiwan. The Space Solver Line was purchased by the company to expand its line of storage and organization products. According to Gary Lee, the company planned to expand the new line through product innovation and make it a more comprehensive and stronger line.

The items in the Space Solver Line were small and had a very high labor content. As a result, the decision was made to import them rather than manufacture them in the U.S. However, the percentage of products imported was relatively small compared to those manufactured at home.

"Many people asked me why did I continue expanding in the U.S. instead of buying more products overseas. We believed we could do a better job with quality, and we believed in American jobs. We believed we wanted to be the best in the world in this business. In retrospect, it was a business risk, and competitive pressures from overseas imports became a huge business challenge.

"It improved the profitability of the company, and really it was the only way you could survive. If I were starting a company today, I'd do something that I never thought I'd say I'd do, and I'd go to China. In today's market, if you are going to compete you are going to have to manufacture in low-cost foreign markets," Des explains.

LEADERS PUT CUSTOMERS FIRST

"Customer service is the name of the game throughout Lee/Rowan. We develop partnerships with all our major customers. We strive to stay close to all our customers and we listen and respond."

– Des Lee

The customer is king. No one believed that more than the founders of Lee/Rowan. Since the very early days when Des' father worked evenings removing rust stains left from the original pants creasers, the company maintained a strong commitment to customer service.

"I had a policy that if anybody had a problem with one of our products, they could send it back, no questions asked. We had a 20-year guarantee on our hangers. You stand behind your product. People would send products back for all kinds of reasons, but we always honored our policy."

And it wasn't just talk, as evidenced by actual customer responses. One customer from Bethlehem, Pennsylvania, wrote, "We are in receipt of the replacement hangers and want to thank you very much for your generosity and understanding. You have restored our faith in American manufacturing by standing behind your product. Your hangers were put to use immediately and so far so good!"

Another satisfied customer notes, "On June 1, 1987, I contacted you by letter concerning a bath towel stand, which had unexplainably broken down. A short time later I was amazed to receive a huge box via UPS. I was even more surprised, indeed pleased, by the contents of the box—a new towel stand to replace the defective one! My companions and I thank you for your kind consideration. By thus standing behind your products, not only have you enhanced your name, but you have also renewed our faith in people. For this, also, we thank you," Sister Paulett.

On March 4, 1996, Helen W. Sheaks wrote, "On February 18 when I received the drying rack you sent me I couldn't have been happier. Many thanks to you. I have been waiting for the bill to come, but apparently one isn't coming. In these times, it is hard to believe that any business firm could be so caring about one customer. I shall be forever grateful and never forget the name Lee/Rowan."

The same attention to service applied to the company's distribution chain. "It was a matter of good dealing. We were progressive. We shipped on time. We had good sales representatives. And we had good people working in our plant."

Additionally, all customers were treated equally regardless of size. It didn't matter to Des whether you were a Wal-Mart and bought lots of products or one of the smaller purchasers; he treated everyone with the same respect and integrity.

"We called on lots of accounts, and they were often tied up with a competitor; but I never lost the determination to keep trying. I kept going to visit them, and they'd be nice. But they weren't interested because they were doing business with one of our competitors. But eventually we won nearly all of them over," Des explains.

Des believes that customer service is the most important element of business. "I learned two rules from Sam Walton. Rule number one: The customer is always right. Rule number two: Refer to rule number one. I always remembered that."

Carole Ritter, Des' longtime assistant, adds that everyone in the company had a clear understanding that customer service was plain old common sense. "You can't buy advertising that cheap. But if someone has had a bad experience with your company and goes to their bridge game and sits down and repeats the story, you wind up with four black eyes."

The following is a poem written by one of the Customer Service Department associates that is indicative of the prevailing attitude.

Here I sit by the telephone, all ready for a ring,
Although you have a problem, we'll solve that awful thing.
The order's in our computer, the info is all there,
And while it takes a little time, all of us do care.
Lee-Rowan loves your business, to us, "you're number one",
We'll follow up and fix it up, until the job is done.

– Pearl Wilson

In 1986, Lee/Rowan instituted a warranty as part of its commitment to quality. Beginning in February of that year, Lee/Rowan products that were sold in boxes carried a label that said the product would be covered by a "full twenty-year warranty." At the time, this was the strongest guarantee of quality ever issued in the industry and meant that the company was willing to replace, without charge, any products that were defective due to material or workmanship within 20 years from the date of purchase. The warranty also appeared on all of the closet accessory items.

"Our company was only able to offer such a warranty because of the commitment to quality shown by every associate within the firm. If you aren't customer-driven, you'll not only lose customers, but you'll also lose the foundation of your business – your people," Des explains.

For many years Lee/Rowan had an Officer's Council made of department and division vice presidents which grew in number as the years progressed. From this point of time the Officers Council was as follows:

Gary Lee, CEO

Dick Rogers President

Bob Luerding, Operations

Ben Jokerst, Secretary/Treasurer

Connie Conrad, Public Relations/Marketing

Ron Moore, Human Resources

Charlie Lammers, Builder's Division

Bill Vesper, Manufacturing

John Godsey, Purchasing

Paul Bertram, Engineering

Jack Schwettman, Jackson Plant Manager

Jim Morley, Retail Division

Margery Lee, Susan Lee, David Lee,
Gary Lee, Elizabeth Lee and Des

Des in 1946, after his Return
from the War

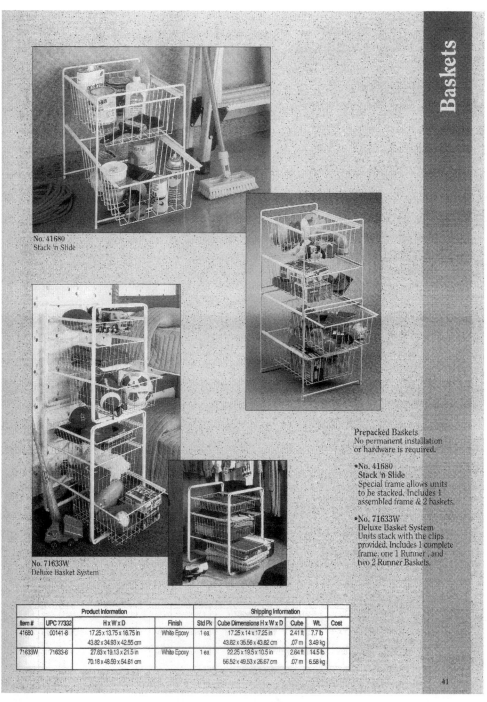

No. 41680
Stack 'n Slide

No. 71633W
Deluxe Basket System

Prepacked Baskets.
No permanent installation
or hardware is required.

•No. 41680
Stack 'n Slide
Special frame allows units
to be stacked. Includes 1
assembled frame & 2 baskets.

•No. 71633W
Deluxe Basket System
Units stack with the clips
provided. Includes 1 complete
frame; one 1 Runner , and
two 2 Runner Baskets.

	Product Information			Shipping Information				
Item #	UPC 77332	H x W x D	Finish	Std Pk	Cube Dimensions H x W x D	Cube	Wt.	Cost
41680	00141-8	17.25 x 13.75 x 16.75 in	White Epoxy	1 ea	17.25 x 14 x 17.25 in	2.41 ft	7.7 lb	
		43.82 x 34.93 x 42.55 cm			43.82 x 35.56 x 43.82 cm	.07 m	3.49 kg	
71633W	71633-6	27.63 x 19.13 x 21.5 in	White Epoxy	1 ea	22.25 x 19.5 x 10.5 in	2.64 ft	14.5 lb	
		70.18 x 48.59 x 54.61 cm			56.52 x 49.53 x 26.67 cm	.07 m	6.58 kg	

41

Lee/Rowan Catalog, 1992

CHAPTER FIVE

LEE/ROWAN: WHERE THE WORLD GETS ORGANIZED.

"I don't know if bigger is better, but the challenges are different. When you start out you it's a matter of survival. But in many industries today you can't remain small because of the nature of merchandizing. You couldn't compete."

– Des Lee

Because of hard work, integrity and innovation, the future looked good for Lee/Rowan. But with growth came new challenges. For Des, who had done just about every job in the company, it meant learning how to be a true chief executive officer and directing a company through the next phases of growth.

"I didn't have any formal training, but I read a lot of business books, which gave me ideas. As the company matured, I matured as a business manager. I became a pretty good CEO, but I learned it the hard way."

BUSINESS OPERATIONS EXPAND

One of the first decisions Des had to make in his new role was where to house the burgeoning operations of the company. The business had no room for growth in its Saint Louis facility so Des had to decide whether to move to a larger location in the city or find an alternative site. He decided to look around for options in other parts of Missouri.

Ultimately, his choice of a location for his second plant was Jackson, Missouri, a nearly 200-year-old town with a population of about six thousand just two hours south of Saint Louis. It was here the company would experience the phenomenal growth that would catapult it into worldwide leadership.

"We were flown to 22 different communities in the state of Missouri in our search for a new location," said Des. "Jackson won out."

Why Jackson? Well, in typical Des Lee fashion, he made the selection because of the quality of the people. "They were genuinely good, hard-working people."

The new plant opened in 1964, and the community had good reason to welcome the newcomer. Lee/Rowan provided jobs and quickly became the largest employer in the area. While the headquarters with its two hundred-plus employees remained in Saint Louis, Des was a frequent visitor to the Jackson plant. He made the trip about once a week with one or two vice-presidents to keep an eye on production, but also to get to know the employees. It was his pleasure, he recalls, to walk through the plant, visiting with the associates.

As the company prospered, Des acquired toy- and furniture-maker Modern Crafts Company of Saint Louis. He wanted to move the company's operations to Jackson, but that would require construction of another plant. Plans were developed for a 53 thousand square-foot facility that would employ an additional 65 employees. However, the plan was contingent upon the passage of a $500 thousand industrial bond issue.

Speaking to a large audience of Jackson Chamber of Commerce members and their spouses at the Wayside Steak House, Des confidently and enthusiastically explained how the facility would double Lee/Rowan's capacity and would further develop the growth of industry in the community. He emphasized that Jackson was a progressive community, and he believed the citizens would not hesitate to vote for the bonds.

They didn't let him down, and the community continued to support him time-and-time again. The company newsletter published glowing reports. First expansion…fifth expansion…groundbreaking and mortgage-burning ceremony… departments revamped for a better future…production is up, up, UP!

Not only was the Jackson plant good for Lee/Rowan operations, but it also attracted the attention of local, state and national officials. In 1986, Missouri Governor John Ashcroft said as he dedicated a new building, "Part of the reason that Missouri is great is because of communities like this one in eastern Missouri, because of the spirit of this county and the willingness of the people here to work together and get the job done in a company such as the one which we celebrate here today.

"People on the East Coast and West Coast call us the fly-over people. But I believe we have something special in Missouri, perhaps characterized best by exactly what we're seeing here today: a spirit of togetherness, a powerful work ethic and the capacity for high technology growth, which I believe is unparalleled elsewhere in this world."

Des Lee couldn't have agreed more. He believed in the people of Jackson, of Missouri, and of America. It was this strong belief that helped guide Lee/Rowan to greatness and would influence Des' decision to give back to the community later in life.

On May 20, 1991, some years after the original groundbreaking in Jackson, the company celebrated the dedication of its ninth expansion. The highlight of the festivities that day included the release of six hundred red, white and blue balloons and a fireworks extravaganza. (Des loves fireworks.) Special daytime pyrotechnics left a trailing American flag in their wake. Of course, there were the company cheers and singing of the company song.

"Lee/Rowan is a great place to be. We make our hangers and shelves for Des Lee. And we are proud to be from Jackson, Missoureeeeee."

But it was not only an opportunity to celebrate the facility's expansion but also to recognize the tremendous success of Lee/Rowan. Because of the company's leadership and the outstanding team of associates, vendors and suppliers, the plant in Jackson had grown from 49,000 square feet to 559,080 square feet. The new addition, added 93,000 square feet of warehouse space. The facility included about 15 acres under roof with more than 1,200 employees in Jackson – a major source of employment for the area.

In 1993, the 10th addition to the Jackson facility was finished. The new building added 81,000 square feet and was dedicated to all the Jackson employees. In June of that same year, another celebration was held in Saint Louis for the renovation of the Saint Louis office and expansion of the Saint Louis facilities. Des' company had come a long way from the rundown office with the tattered furniture, crude machinery and tools, and soot-stained windows.

Finally, the company grew so large that it reached full capacity in Saint Louis and Jackson. With no more room for expansion, the company bought a facility in Newbern, Tennessee. The Newbern location was chosen once again, in typical Des Lee fashion, because of the community itself.

"There was a great work ethic there, much like I had found in Jackson and Saint Louis. Plus the community is conveniently located just 45 minutes from Jackson and less than three hours from Saint Louis," Des explained.

The Newbern facility had 252,000 square feet and was situated on 22 acres making it suitable for expansion when necessary. The plant was to be used to manufacture wire shelving and would initially employ about one hundred people. Long-range plans called for a workforce of over three hundred at this location with no decrease in workforces in either of the other plants. But the Newbern facility never opened because Des would make the decision to sell Lee/Rowan before it became operational.

As an example of the employees' company spirit, two customer service associates wrote the following poem.

Ode to Lee/Rowan

Written and performed by Laverne Keating and Mary Field

It's a pleasure to come and talk about Lee/Rowan
And give you some facts that keep us growing.

The Company got started back in '39
By a man who was truthful, honest and kind.

The employee count has soared over these 52 years
With Des at the head, who takes away the "unemployment" fears.

Every person is special and has a certain job,
So on Thursday we can get paid and don't have to sob.

No one department can build the company without the others,
So why not treat each other as your sister's and brothers.

We are all special and must keep our head high,
And watch Lee/Rowan sales and profits reach toward the sky.

We pull and work together to make this Lee/Rowan team
When we have finished product, we look at it and beam.

Each department plays a position on this team.
All players are needed if you know what I mean.

We must go out and sell quality products to the buyers,
Proving we are number one, and not just liars.

As you walk through the stores and see our display's a mess,
Straighten them up and make OURs look their very best.

We must all be conscious of the quality and service we provide,
As we mention Lee/Rowan and see the "sparkle" in the customer's eye.

We must strive to keep our prices in line and our quality high
So our customers won't buy the imports and tell us bye bye.

Speak up with your ways and ideas to save money in everything you do.
So you'll get bigger profit sharing checks...made payable to you!

As years pass we see new faces and teach them our Lee/Rowan song.
Lee/Rowan will continue to be strong, and go on and on.

Lee/Rowan Cheerleaders at the Jackson, Missouri Plant Dedication

LEADERS INVEST IN THE POWER OF PEOPLE

"We believe people are our most important asset. We have a constant, sincere and caring concern for our people which we believe is essential to produce teamwork, innovation and growth."

– Des Lee

The essence of leadership comes not only from the ability to design strategy but also from the ability to lead with your heart. Truly great leaders can ignite passion and inspire others to see their vision. They instill values, and they can move people toward shared dreams. They challenge people to be the best they can be. In others words, true leaders trust people to do their jobs.

Today, there are volumes of published literature on how to become an effective leader, and management programs teach leadership skills. But when Des Lee stepped up to the position of president at Lee/Rowan, he knew very little about management theory.

"I was a graduate of business school, but back then they didn't teach you anything about that. It was all theory," he explains. Furthermore, at the time Des was named president, companies had yet to discover the concepts of teams and empowerment. Many continued to function under a strict hierarchical structure with employees who could easily be characterized as the classic company man.

Intuitively, however, Des understood the importance of human capital. The elder Lee set the tone for good employee relations, and Des absorbed his father's philosophy. Des knew everyone on the premises. His days were filled with a mixture of thinking up ideas for new products, designing those products, and making the rounds of every department and the factory floor, asking employees how their families were doing.

His ability to connect with people, which he had displayed in his childhood, emerged again in this arena, and he excelled. A step ahead of his time, he never referred to the people who worked at Lee/Rowan as employees, they were always "associates." And he never believed in isolating himself in an ivory tower.

"I started to work as a clerk in the purchasing department in 1956," recalled Mary Lou Schwedemann. "We purchased wire and chemicals and gold. I was told that first day that I was to meet Mr. Lee and I was scared to death because I was the newest kid on the block. But it didn't take long to stop worrying. He was great. Then, when my son was born, Des was so interested. He has been like a guardian angel," she shared.

"When Des would go to the plant," Carole Ritter says, "he would go down the line and talk to people about their families. They always loved it. He knew them, and he knew things to talk to them about. It made him a real person."

"I have heard so many people, even in small companies, say, 'The hell with the employees,'" Des said. "They take advantage of them, and it just makes me sick to my stomach to hear that. It's so different from my own basic philosophy."

Des' true commitment and belief in people is reflected in a holiday message he wrote for the company newsletter in 1981.

> *I think one of the greatest biblical passages in The Bible is from the book of Matthew, where Jesus was confronted by the Pharisees, who asked him what were the greatest Commandments. His answer was "You shall love the Lord, your God, with all your heart, with all your soul and with all your mind. The second was "Thy shall love thy neighbor as thy self."*
>
> *This pretty well tells the whole story of the Christian Faith, which started with the birth of Jesus – whose birthday we celebrate as Christmas. Christ's teachings have transcended mankind's struggles for over 2,000 years, and the principals are as sound today as they were when he spoke them.*
>
> *Our fellow employees are, in a sense, our neighbors, and we should work together as a team supporting one another in our common goal to provide a living and a better way of life for each of us. We all come from different backgrounds and are certainly different in appearance, color, beliefs and desires. But we all, as employees, have one thing in common – Lee/Rowan is the basis of our unity.*

Determined not to be a dictatorial business leader, Des maintained an open door policy. He believed a strict bureaucratic organization would ruin a company, and he was determined not to allow layers upon layers of management. He created a flat organization.

"People felt comfortable coming in and challenging me. Everybody, anybody could come in, and they did. I'd always listen and be open to what they had to say," Des said.

His desire to maintain a caring, open, flat organization was the impetus behind his strong fight to keep the union out of his company. The Boilermaker's Union tried to organize the plant in Saint Louis, and Des was disappointed and disheartened, but definitely not defeated.

"The union hosted inside meetings where they served ham sandwiches and beer. You always have a certain amount of dissatisfaction in any organization. My best informer was the janitor. He always told me what was going on. He would come into my office and close the door, and we would talk.

"When the union came in, I was so upset I couldn't sleep at night. I was scared. I was trying to keep the company together, and here was another layer of management coming on threatening to disrupt everything. I couldn't afford that. I knew they didn't have the employees' interest at heart.

"We had always been good to everyone. If I didn't have them on my side, if we were not working together, we would not succeed. I couldn't do it on my own. By nature, I wanted to work with people. I wanted to collaborate," he explains.

Des called the employees all together and he held up his fist and told them, "I will fight fire with fire. I will close the plant rather than let the union come in."

But the union did come in and fortunately, Des didn't make good on his threat to close the plant. Des sued the union to force a decision on who could vote in the decertification election to eliminate the union. He lost the case in the lower courts, but appealed all the way to the U.S. Supreme Court, determined to win the issue. Then, the employees took another vote, and the union was out.

Des also understood the importance of leading by example and with integrity and a strong sense of values. "You can't get people to work for you and give you their best unless you are honest with them." The best way to motivate people, he adds, is through the personality of the leader. "I'm not an overly intelligent person; I'm a very average person. But I have good people skills and because of that, I think I could run just about any type of company."

Following the example his father set years ago when he stressed fairness and concern in evaluating his students, Des was a demanding, yet fair and compassionate boss. Committed to maintaining quality people on his team, associates could only be dismissed with the approval of Des or his son and right arm, Gary.

Additionally, Des believed in sharing information with all the Lee/Rowan associates. There were annual award banquets and annual meetings with staff to report earnings, capital expenditures, marketing plans and profit-sharing results.

"Everybody in the company knew how much money we made. We shared the numbers, we shared everything," Des added. "We tried to create friendliness and motivate people to work together as a team."

The goal was to instill a sense of entrepreneurship throughout the company. Des believed he could do that by making every single individual feel part of the bottom line results of the company.

At every opportunity, Des made sure Lee/Rowan associates were recognized, both professionally and personally. Birthdays were announced over the public address system daily. Personal notes were sent to associates who were ill or bereaved.

"And every year at Christmas time, everybody in the company got a ham, even if it was your first day on the job," adds Carole Ritter.

While there was no formal tuition reimbursement program like many companies have today, Des made sure a lot of people had the opportunity to go to school. "All we'd say is that it must be in some way related to your position, so we're not paying to educate them for nothing. If you believe in your people, most of them will do the right thing."

A hefty investment was also made in employee training and development programs. "We offered courses through AAIM – American Association of Industrial Management – to our associates to help them better their skills," he explained

The training classes were popular among the associates at Lee/Rowan. For example, a course called "Managing for Results" sold out for the first session, so it had to be offered a second time.

In addition to training courses, Des and his management team would host meetings in the factories. "We wanted to acquaint every single person in the company with everything we could. We weren't professional trainers, but we did our best, and we constantly encouraged everyone within the organization to learn and to grow," adds Des.

Team spirit was strong at the company – a sentiment nurtured and fostered from the highest offices. Perhaps because of Des' love of team sports, company pep rallies, complete with cheerleaders and a company marching song, added to the esprit de corps. Frequently, Des would be right in the middle playing his drums and singing along as the enthusiastic group sang: (to the tune of "When the Saints Go Marching In")

We are a team, Lee/Rowan team
Storage systems is our theme.
We associates pull together,
We are a strong Lee/Rowan team.

"I enjoyed the people. Everyone worked as a team, as one big family."
– Bettye Blevins (1981)

LEADERS ARE GREAT COMMUNICATORS

"Our employees take charge of their individual jobs as if they each own the company."

– Des Lee

Calling Des a great communicator would be a vast understatement. He's better than great. A 1991 newspaper article noted that only 34 percent of employees responding to a survey believe their company really listens to them, and they indicated only ten percent of CEOs communicate effectively with their organizations. However, the article put Des at the top of the list of great communicators. He was cited as one of the best, even after 52 years with Lee/Rowan.

"Des still spends more than ten percent of this time walking through the plant, talking with employees and spending many hours talking with all levels of our office staff," explained Dick Rogers, a former Lee/Rowan president.

"In addition to Lee/Rowan's open-door policy, there is a telephone hot line, and any associate can use a "Talk-Up" form to write confidentially to Des, asking questions, airing problems or voicing opinions. Des always provides a prompt response," he continued.

"No one was in a better position to make suggestions about improving our productivity, work methods, cost savings, quality, safety, customer service and new products than the people who worked to make our products," Des explained. "I wanted to encourage everyone to participate in making the company a better place to work and to make our products better for our customers."

Lee/Rowan also launched its SPIRIT program in 1984. The purpose of the program was to increase productivity, improve attendance and safety and to share the savings that resulted from those improvements. All associates shared in the success of the program. Associates earned spirit points, which could be redeemed for high quality merchandise from a gift catalog.

The number of long-term employees at Lee/Rowan is perhaps the most significant tribute to the company's culture. For example, at the 1992 awards banquet, when many companies were struggling with high turnover rates, Mary Lou Schwendemann was recognized for 36 years of service; 26 associates were recognized for 15-20 years of service; and another 28 employees had worked for the company for 10 to 15 years. Each was recognized for being an integral part of the team.

"Des loved the people who worked in the company and they loved him," says Carole Ritter.

Nurturing the team concept was critical to Des and to the success of Lee/Rowan – so important that Des considered himself part of the team. For example, there were no reserved parking spots for anyone at the company – including Des.

LEADERS HIRE THE RIGHT PEOPLE WITH THE RIGHT STUFF.

"Motivating people is the most important skill any executive can possess."

—Des Lee

Long before Tom Peters, Peter Drucker and other management gurus wrote about the importance of building diverse teams to address complex business challenges, Des Lee had it figured out.

Bill Vesper had retired after 40 years with the Hussman Corporation, but realized he wasn't ready to fade off into the sunset. Vesper was introduced to Lee/Rowan through acquaintances. "I had received some job offers after my retirement, but had taken no serious interviews because I didn't want to start a new job on the rebound." A meeting with Des Lee convinced Vesper to begin working at Lee/Rowan.

"Des is a person who works with people, which is my style of management. He's an executive who is genuinely interested in his employees and their welfare," said Bill Vesper, vice president of manufacturing

Connie Conrad, who became the company's vice president of marketing, had a similar experience. "I wasn't looking for a job when he recruited me. He called every person by name, and they wanted to talk to him. They reached out to him. I thought, 'I want to work for this man.' He's one of the most incredible human beings I've met in my life."

"I always hired people who were smarter than me, and I believe it is important to have a diverse team," Des explains. "Progress comes through diverse opinions and ideas. Even those individuals you consider mavericks can often be converted into major contributors."

Des also notes it is important to have people who fit the culture of your organization and share your values. "Looking back over the years, there were a few individuals who I should have gotten rid of, but I kept thinking I could change them. But I learned you can't change people," Des notes.

Much like raising children, Des believed in being firm but fair with everyone. And one of the biggest lessons he learned is that no matter what you do for your employees, you will never hit 100 percent.

"I tried to motivate the employees and make them feel part of the team. I wanted them to feel important in the company and to challenge them to use their intellect, their creativity, their imagination and their work ethics, but I never got 100 percent.

"I always believed in empowerment. Regardless of any human relations policy a company has, it is of little value unless the leaders are caring, sincere and sensitive.

"But you can't baby employees. You want employees, in addition to receiving a paycheck, to have self-esteem, and you want them to feel they have made a contribution.

"We are all different. I don't think anyone's philosophy should be a guide for anyone else's philosophy. We are all individuals and should do what we feel comfortable doing," Des explains.

LEADERS ARE EARLY ADAPTERS

At the turn of the Twentieth Century, Charles Duell served as the director of the U.S. Patent Office. He recommended closing the office because he believed everything that could possibly be invented had already been done. Imagine how foolish he might feel today if he could see the amazing technological advances introduced in the Twentieth Century, and he would undoubtedly be awed at the speed at which they continue.

Those who insulate themselves in a cocoon-like attitude of "this is the way we've always done it" create a death knell for their companies. True leaders have an ability to see the future with its myriad possibilities, and they readily accept and embrace change. Throughout the history of Lee/Rowan, Des had been able to flex the direction of the company to keep pace with changing markets. However, as the world began to shift from the industrial age to the information age in the late 1970s, a new challenge appeared: Technology.

Technology literally transformed the way all business around the world was conducted and many companies were hesitant to buy into the new-fangled machines. Des, who maintains he still doesn't know how to turn a computer on and off, nonetheless, recognized the changing environment and stepped out in front to ensure his company was positioned to take advantage of the enhanced productivity and profitability new technology would mean. He astutely recognized the difference between possessing technological gizmos and actually using them to enhance business practices.

"I was always looking for ways to do things better. So I made sure we invested in the kind of equipment that could enhance the quality of our product and increase our productivity," says Des.

Focusing on the concerns of the Lee/Rowan associates, Des was quick to alleviate fears that automation and additional technology would replace people. "Our associates should not be alarmed as we install automatic equipment to replace hand operations, because our history has shown that as we continue to automate, we grow and provide additional employment. In other words, automation at Lee/Rowan has definitely improved job security," Des noted in 1985.

Early adaptations were made to incorporate technology into the manufacturing process including the automation of skirt and blouse Add-A-Hangers as well as rebuilding of the plating equipment making it one of the most modern in the nation. Many of the automation enhancement ideas and suggestions came from the company's cost reduction committees.

"A machine operator is likely to be the best person to point out a possible improvement because he or she knows the best way to arrange the material and perform the operation. Likewise, a warehouseman or material handler is the best individual to suggest method changes on the job since they are actually performing the jobs themselves. All of these associates' suggestions were vitally important in order for the company to constantly reduce our costs and improve our operations and products. Our primary goal was to provide our customers with a competitively priced, quality product," Des explained

Lee/Rowan associates were so enthusiastic and focused on the company's mission that one machine – designed to aid in the manufacture and assembly of products – was developed, designed and tooled completely in-house. Associate Gene McAtee developed the concept and prototype of a machine that fed in balls and wires automatically and welded the balls to the wire for the over-the-door towel racks.

Then, Bob Tabers from the company's Design Department utilized computer assisted design rather than tedious hand drawings to draw up the plans for the machine. All the components for the machine were made in the Saint Louis tool room. Another associate, Ralph Green, was responsible for the installation and design of the electrical components. Once again, an all-in-the-family, Lee/Rowan success.

Additionally, a computer-programmed automatic hoist plating machine was added to the plating department in the early 1980s.

Significantly outpacing its competitors, Lee/Rowan introduced computers throughout the company by 1984. "Although originally computers were thought of as somewhat of a nuisance, they became a vital part of the company," explains Gary Lee, former CEO of the company.

Utilizing computers in the customer service department to enhance the company's efforts to provide unmatched customer service was a top priority of Des'. Computers also improved coordination and service for the shipping departments. The shipping departments at both plants – Saint Louis and Jackson – had to work together closely. Their responsibility was to see that orders were shipped out on time and in good condition which involved "staying on top of the freight lines," according to Jackson General Manager of Shipping Wayne Brim. The new technology allowed the process to go much more smoothly.

Without the fast acceptance of technology throughout Lee/Rowan, Des' story may have had a very different ending. But his leadership and vision allowed the company to adapt and adjust its operations and, accordingly, continue to grow and expand.

Des Lee on Engine Number Five in Jackson, Missouri, 1965

CHAPTER SIX

LEADERS BRING STYLE AND SUBSTANCE

"We are living in a dynamic era of history. I am convinced there needs to be a change in the corporate atmosphere to stimulate more entrepreneurial type thinking."

– Des Lee

LEADERS SHARE THEIR PASSION

Perched atop an old steam locomotive sits Des Lee decked out in his railroad conductor's uniform – not exactly the typical attire for the chairman of an international multimillion-dollar enterprise – as he poses for a picture for the cover of a national trade magazine. But then again, there is nothing typical about Des Lee.

Des admits he loves nothing more than to don his engineer's overalls with a red bandanna and climb into the cab to pilot the train on its short journey from Jackson toward the main line in Delta, Missouri. In fact, no one could ever see a happier face in a photograph than is on the cover the June 15, 1992 issue of HFD, The Weekly Home Furnishing Newspaper (copyright 1992 by Fairchild Publications, a Capital Cities/ABC, Inc. company).

Decked out in full engineer's regalia, Des, smiling with his boyish charm, is pictured in front of Old Number Five, a steam locomotive in Jackson. And the story begins: "As the steam locomotive Shelby Brown pulled out of the Saint Louis Iron Mountain & Southern Railway terminal, the Coyote Creek Bluegrass Band on board the train plucked out the opening notes to 'Oh, Susanna' and Des picked up a washboard and scratched along. No self-impressed, stuffed shirt CEO."

Des always loved trains. He owned his first Lionel model when he was a child, and he built a scale model engine actually powered with live steam. He put it together with four thousand parts imported from Japan. These parts are now displayed in the Mercantile

Library on the University of Missouri-Saint Louis Campus.

"It was such a success that we had four or five parties in the next few years. I would have over-the-road motor coaches, and the guests would gather on a parking lot in Saint Louis on a Sunday afternoon. When they arrived at the train depot in Jackson, we would have a bar set up inside the train with snacks, and we would have entertainment on the train. It would be about a 45-minute ride on the train," notes Carole Ritter.

About 20 minutes into the train ride, however, Des' guests would be surprised by a staged holdup. Carole says, "A bunch of masked train robbers on horseback would board the train and kidnap some of the passengers and take them into the park where the party would be set up."

The day ended with a big picnic dinner under an enormous tent and was always topped off with a flamboyant fireworks display. Carole says, "Des likes boomers, and I like the 'ooh-ahs' so we have mostly boomers with 'ooh-ahs' in between."

But even with Carole's meticulous event planning, Des' parties didn't always go smoothly.

"At one time, we were dedicating a plant expansion and dignitaries, including Governor Christopher "Kit" Bond, were to be our special guests. I went down early to help and make sure the bunting and other decorations were in place and the food preparation was on schedule. A few hours before the event, I had a call from the hotel saying it had heard from the health department, and their kitchen would be closed.

"We had invited all the county commissioners, so I called their office and said I needed to talk right away to the chief county official. I got him on the phone and explained what was happening and, in a panic, asked him what could I do?

"He told me not to worry about a thing, and he'd call me right back. He was sure it was a big mistake," Carole remembers.

"Well, it was a mistake. It turned out to be a practical joke on the part of one of the hotel's competitors, but it nearly gave me a heart attack," she adds.

No one was able to escape Des' enthusiasm and love for the old ironsides. Following the 1987 dedication ceremony of a new plant addition, Governor John Ashcroft was "kidnapped" off the train by a sheriff's posse and released at a city park where several hundred guests greeted him for his birthday celebration. These special events were so important to Des that six weeks after he had had a six-way heart bypass, he insisted on attending a scheduled party. The only concession was his agreement to allow his wife to drive him the two hours south to Jackson instead of riding the bus with the rest of the guests. Like his attitude toward business, nothing was going to stand in his way of getting to where he wanted to go.

In many respects, Des' love of trains is more than fun and games; it is symbolic of a thought-provoking view on our evolving culture.

"In any changing culture, you discard a lot of beautiful things in order to accommodate new ways. I have a strong feeling that we are always moving toward a period of great enlightenment. I do not think that will change human nature, but we should hope that we can learn to live together better than we have in the past and that we can accomplish greater things."

Leaders, like Des, are willing to share themselves. They are not icons to be watched from afar, but real people with passions and a zest for life.

LEADING WITH PRINCIPLES, VALUES AND INTEGRITY

"You can accomplish anything in life, provided that you do not mind who gets the credit."

– Harry Truman

The greatness of an organization is not equal to the sum of its parts – the sum of its parts is greater than the whole. Each individual brings strength and perception. When combined with the others within the company, the end result is a much stronger entity. A successful organization does not evolve from the efforts of one person – but rather from the minds and hearts of every person involved.

That kind of commitment from employees comes when they feel a sense of respect and appreciation – where there is a sense of integrity and values. Values and integrity originate from the top of the organization chart – with a strong commitment from management. It has been said that gifted leadership begins where heart and head – feeling and thought – meet. Leaders who are self-absorbed and impressed with themselves never reach greatness.

"Employees must be able to know where you stand so you must provide consistent, predictable and sincere leadership every single day," Des says. They must be able to depend upon you and know what you stand for. They must also be allowed to risk failure without fear of reprimands."

An effective leader obtains the commitment to a clear and compelling vision, which in turn stimulates higher performance standards. Des believed in setting high standards for all the Lee/Rowan associates, but no higher than those he set for himself. "Most employees want a challenge and aspire to grow. If they know what is expected of them and they are given the opportunity to be a part of a team, they will excel. People want their contributions and ideas to be recognized, to make a difference

To accomplish that goal, Des stressed the importance of constantly communicating the company's common goals, mission and beliefs. One of the biggest reasons for business failure is management's inability to adopt, communicate and focus this information throughout the organization.

Like his friend Sam Walton, Des is a proponent of managing by walking around. "Let your people know that you are interested in what they are doing and that you genuinely care. You can't overdo this, but the key is being genuine."

Additionally, Des stresses the importance of avoiding the damaging effect of a strict bureaucratic hierarchy. Bureaucracy is the greatest enemy of entrepreneurism. You want employees to feel empowered, and you never want to reprimand them for thinking creatively or suggesting new ideas or ways of doing business.

Since the early days of Lee/Rowan when the four founders utilized their varied skills to launch a successful business, Des has emphasized the importance of embracing diverse skills, abilities and personality types.

Finally, Des believes it's important to encourage people to have fun. As Teddy Roosevelt once stated, "If you find a job you enjoy doing, you will never work a day in your life."

But most importantly, Des lived by what he called his Ten Commandments of Effective Selling. These commandments reflect the high moral standards of the man and his business leadership.

1. Practice the highest standards of integrity with your company and your customers at all times.
2. Have a thorough knowledge of your products, their features, their strengths, their advantages, their uses and pricing.
3. Know your competition, their products, their strengths, their weaknesses, their market strategy, their pricing. Never underestimate them. Never discredit them.
4. Sell your company's culture, its values, its philosophy, its policies and its successes.
5. Earn the right to increased sales through relentless determination, perseverance, hard work and continuous learning.
6. Be on time for all appointments. Keep all commitments.
7. Constantly cultivate new customers.
8. Make prompt follow-up on any complaints or problems. Stay involved.
9. Live out your selling philosophy in everything you do. Don't limit it to customers alone.
10. Don't oversell or pressure your customers. Play for the long haul.

"I never had any ethics courses, and I assumed people who ran businesses were ethical because I didn't know any better. There hadn't been any great national scandals in the business world. I didn't know people were selfish or greedy," Des said.

He is quick to note that a lack of integrity today is damaging our capitalistic system. "There is too much disparity between what the top corporate executives are getting and what the average employee is getting. It is almost ridiculous and a poison to the system. It is unthinkable that these people would do this. As businesses get bigger and bigger, they have lost sight of what is important. Most importantly, they have lost sight that it's all about the people. Without good, quality people, you have no business," he adds.

Too many companies are willing to pay top executives anything if they can improve the bottom line. But these executives can't possibly do it on their own. Ultimately to be successful, these executives must be leaders of people. "That's the only way you're going to motivate people to give their best efforts, talent and energy," Des notes. "If we don't correct some of the inequities in our capitalistic system, eventually the American Dream will be dead."

Jackson, Missouri Plant
Epoxy Coating Line

Rolls of Wire in
Jackson, Missouri Plant

Des entertains Guests at a Train Ride Party in Cape Girardeau, Missouri

73

Des Lee recieves the Housewares Club Hall of Fame Award in Boston - 1988

CHAPTER SEVEN

TRANSITIONS

LEADERS ARE ALSO GREAT TEACHERS

Following in his father's footsteps, Gary Lee began working for Lee/Rowan in production during the summers. While doing regular production jobs, he dug a hole for a punch press foundation and unloaded lumber to be used in sandboxes for the toy division. After graduating from Texas Christian University with a degree in business administration, Gary worked in the sales department of Jones and Laughlin Steel Company. In 1971, he joined the sales team at Lee/Rowan. Quickly, he proved his prowess in sales, and he was promoted to national sales manager of the toy division.

"When I started at Lee/Rowan, we had two divisions – housewares and toys. Eventually, I became head of the toy division, which was, at that time, a $4 million-plus business," Gary explained. "Then I was promoted to vice president of sales with responsibility for sales of all products."

"Gary was a great salesman," Des says of his son. "Gary had the vision to see the volume opportunities in the mass market. He realized that as a company, we couldn't remain competitive and continue to sell only to department stores."

"We started at zero but built it up until we were the largest manufacturer, selling 100 thousand shelving feet a year," added Gary.

Des' daughter, Christy, joined the company in the early 1980s. She stayed for one year in the Lee/Rowan sales department, but left to pursue her career in art. Upon her departure, Gary took on additional responsibilities.

In 1981 Gary was elected executive vice president of the company and on July 6, 1984, Gary was named president of Lee/Rowan by the board of directors. Des remained active in all phases of the business as chairman of the board and chief executive officer.

Des said at the time, "I have no intention of retiring since this company has always been a vital and challenging part of my life. And I look forward to Lee/Rowan growing and prospering with Gary as president."

Watching Gary mature in various positions of responsibility, Des provided a subtle guiding hand. But like all of the associates at Lee/Rowan, Des allowed his son latitude to learn to lead in his own way.

"Gary had a rare marketing instinct and an ability to gauge the future of this industry. He understood consumer demand and made vital decisions, which spurred the company's growth," Des noted.

Gary was strongly influenced by his father's philosophy of business. He too was a strong believer in team spirit and had an innate sense of integrity. Des knew the company was in good hands.

Supporting his son in his new role, Des said in remarks to the Lee/Rowan associates, "Even though Gary is a part of the Lee family, he was, more importantly, a member of the Lee/Rowan company family and has been since birth," Des stated. "The growth of Lee/Rowan is a part of his heritage."

"I am confident that Gary's drive and enthusiasm along with his determination and marketing skills will prove invaluable in his leadership and in furthering the growth of our company."

BUSINESS SUCCESS – PERSONAL CHALLENGES

Under Des' leadership, Lee/Rowan had experienced phenomenal growth – greater than the young Jimmy Rowan and Des Lee's early entrepreneurial dreams. In 1970, the firm had expanded into bath furniture, and in 1985 it developed the Storage Systems ventilated wire product line. There was a big 50th anniversary celebration in 1989, and the purchase of the Space Solvers line in 1990. A new Under Cabinet Organizer Line appeared on the market in 1991 followed by Sports and Lawn Organizers, Solid Oak Shelving and Max-Track adjustable shelving in 1992.

A slick, four-color catalog offered a whole family of innovative products and cited the company's growth from a one-product manufacturer to a multi-dimensional corporation. Pictured was an incredible array of tension pole systems, bath organizers, open storage shelving, oak and wire shelving, baskets, door/wall racks, under-cabinet organizers, locker organizers, accessory organizers, ventilated organizers, show racks, space solvers, hangers of every description – more than 600 products, the wire and wood descendants of those first pants creasers fashioned in the dilapidated building on the Saint Louis riverfront. Many of these products were the creations of Des Lee and his almost daily effort to design, change or adapt innovative products.

Lee/Rowan was no longer a mom-and-pop operation. It was an international market leader in the storage systems industry. Over the years, the company had driven several aggressive conglomerate competitors out of business. The company's success was undeniable, and in 1991, Des Lee was inducted in to the Entrepreneurs Hall of Fame at the sixth annual "Entrepreneurs Hall of Fame and Salute to Buyers" tribute dinner in Boston. Sponsored by the Housewares Club of New England, the event honors those entrepreneurs whose individual style of leadership takes their companies to new heights of national recognition in their industries. It is only natural that Des would have been included. Over the past 10 years, the company had grown 400 percent. Des had become recognized nationwide as a speaker on the spirit of entrepreneurism, and the company culture he had built by making every associate at Lee/Rowan a part of the team was enviable as was his unmatched customer service commitment.

Even with such a prestigious recognition, however, Des struggled with the self-doubt and insecurities that had haunted him since childhood, along with issues involving the growth and profitability of the company. He slipped into an almost paralyzing depression accompanied by a painful and debilitating bout of shingles. His thousands of acquaintances who don't know him well would find it hard to believe that this friendly, casual, seemingly self-assured man could fall victim to serious depression. But he gives the troubling mental problem some of the credit for his success.

"I remember going to work every day and not feeling competent or qualified to accept the responsibilities for running the company," Des admits. It was his faithful assistant Carole who kept encouraging him.

"I was under constant stress," he adds. "I couldn't escape the anxiety and the mounting competitive challenges."

Emerson Electric Corporation, a major Saint Louis company, purchased Lee/Rowan's main competitor Clarison. Clarison was larger than Lee/Rowan, but Des' company was beginning to surpass it. Now, however, Clarison had the backing of a huge corporation with deep pockets.

Des remembers calling Emerson's CEO Chuck Knight to welcome him to the industry. "He did not respond to my call. That said to me he thought I was so insignificant that I wasn't worth bothering with. Then I heard that Emerson was going to build a plant in Mexico, which we couldn't afford to do. I also heard that they had hired an MBA from Harvard as the new marketing director. All this depressed and frightened me even more."

Lee/Rowan associates began to notice a difference in their leader, and they became concerned. Carole assured them it was nothing more than a slow recovery from a bout with the flu; however, there were days when Des was unable to dictate, concentrate or make a decision.

"I've never experienced any illness like mental depression. I finally called my doctor after several weeks and told him I needed help. He put me on medication and explained that one out of ten people, particularly people of my temperament, suffer from depression at some time in their life – even people like Churchill and other world leaders. It was a turning point for me when I realized I was not alone, and there was no disgrace or weakness due to my illness."

During this time, Des took many long walks and spent time evaluating his life. As he recovered, he came to grips with the most difficult decision of his life. He decided to sell the business.

"When you own your own company, you call your own shots. Your company is an expression of your own vision. You have a chance to be the employer of your people and affect their lives. You can do anything you want to do within your own realm of financial resources."

And it was the issue of financial resources that was handicapping Lee/Rowan. Merging with a larger firm might have been an option or taking the company public, neither of which appealed to the unfettered entrepreneur.

"We did merge with several small companies through the years, but I never wanted to take Lee/Rowan public. If you want to go big-time, you go public; I didn't see it as a business that would attract enough capital and sustain a good enough return on investment for a long enough period of time. Plus, I wanted to control my own destiny, and you can't do that when you take a company public," Des explained.

In addition to the company's financial issues, personal financial security was also in the back of Des' mind. Even though his firm had prospered, and he was in a comfortable financial situation, he was not a wealthy man, and he was not in the elite echelon of the Saint Louis movers and shakers who could sign six-figure checks for their favorite charities or community organizations. From boyhood, he had to watch pennies. As his income increased, he learned to watch dollars. He wanted to make sure his children never had to struggle and would always be financially secure.

"Selling the company seemed to be the only way I knew to ensure there would be a nest egg for my children," Des confided.

After weighing all the choices, Des realized it was time to sell. Newell Company, a manufacturing conglomerate based in Freeport, Illinois, had been courting Lee/Rowan for a couple of years. Des was ready to talk turkey.

Negotiations began and, as you might expect, one of Des' foremost concerns was for the welfare of the Lee/Rowan associates. He may have given the impression that he was a good old country boy, but as the sharp negotiator he turned out to be, he insisted that neither the profit-sharing plan he had instituted nor his already committed gifts would be affected by the sale. Some of the Newell executives commented that Des was the toughest negotiator they had ever worked with.

Another aspect of the sale that was difficult for Des was that his son was an integral part of the family business and at the time, was serving as the company's CEO.

"At first Gary was upset, and I understand that. But I knew it was the best decision. He stayed on for a while with the new organization, but now he has his own business and is doing very well," says Des.

On September 23, 1993, in the few seconds it took to sign the closing papers, he closed the door on a career that carried him from a financially strapped, struggling young man in the Depression to the chairman of a multi-million-dollar international company. He exited a very wealthy man. The price tag for the privately held enterprise was $75 million plus assuming $25 million of debt for a total of $100 million.

Des' executive assistant Carole remembers the day the check made out to Des arrived at the bank. "They said at the time it was the largest check they had ever seen written to an individual."

Lee/Rowan, which for decades had been a family operation, now was one of nearly 20 divisions. "They eventually closed the Saint Louis plant, which was a good thing to do. I probably would have had to do that sooner or later, but I had no idea of doing that at the time we were sold because I was concerned about those employees. I didn't know how many of them would be willing to move to Jackson to work in our plant there," Des explained.

Free of the stress and challenge of the day-to-day business world and with his pockets lined with gold, Des had another decision to make: What would he do with the rest of his life. Initially the answer seemed obvious. During the negotiations, the buyer had indicated that Des would be a consultant for two years. He had looked forward to visiting shows and perhaps, suggesting new products. It was a great way to wean himself from the hustle-and-bustle of running the firm. But the opportunity didn't materialize, and Des quickly began to feel unwanted and unneeded. One month after the sale was completed, he received a telephone call from headquarters asking him to clear out his office in two weeks and vacate the premises.

Sadly, he had to accept the fact that he was no longer part of Lee/Rowan. (Gary was retained as president of the new corporation.) But as Carole and Des cleaned out his office, Des began to ponder his next move. While he might have been physically gone, Des Lee would remain forever in the hearts and minds of all the Lee/Rowan associates,

Des Lee recieves Honorary Doctorate of Humane Letters from Washington University

Des and Mary Ann Lee/Des recieved the Honorary Humanitarian Award from University of Missouri - St. Louis

Des Lee, UM-St. Louis Chancellor Emeritus Blanche M. Touhill and
Wm. Orthwein, Jr. at a Press Conference announcing the Formation of
the Des Lee Collaborative Vision

Chapter Eight

Leaders are Benevolent

"If our community is to prosper in this rapidly changing world, we must be a city that embraces change using every ounce of our vision, talent and resources."

– Des Lee

any fondly refer to Des Lee as Mr. Generosity, and generous he is. As a wealthy man, Des could have decided to take it easy for a while and enjoy the good life. But staying at home and fading into the sunset held no lure for this dynamic, creative man. Des began to consider his options.

One challenge he confronted was how to manage the money he had received from the sale of Lee/Rowan. A heavy tax bill loomed before him, and the thought of giving away his hard-earned dollars to the government wasn't appealing. Using his innovative and creative thinking skills, Des searched for an option. After doing some research he came up with a solution that would not only minimize his tax bill, but also allow him to do something he had always wanted to do – make a difference in his community. To the astonishment of many and the gratitude of others, Des decided to give his money away and launch his second career.

Of course, Des didn't truly set out to give all of his money away. "I want to feel secure financially. That is why I don't want to give away all my money. I have been struggling all my life, but I can't see, beyond passing along a reasonable amount to my children, whom I have provided for with insurance policies, why I shouldn't take a good portion of what I have and help the community and those less fortunate," he explains. "This would give me more personal inward satisfaction than anything else I can do."

While the tax consequences of charitable giving are undisputed, Des' motivation is more deeply personal than financial. He does it because he believes in the importance of giving back and has always been willing to give, even when he was not a wealthy man.

"I have always wanted to be involved in trying to make things better. Early on, I was involved with a hearing and speech center. I saw families there who didn't have any money, whose children needed speech therapy. It was important to do something for them," Des explained.

The commitment to help others has been a motivational force in Des Lee's life for many years. Both of his parents instilled in him the importance of helping others. He was also profoundly affected by the bigotry and cruelty black soldiers endured during World War II.

"When I returned from overseas where I had seen death and destruction, I made a commitment to myself that I would try to do something worthwhile with my life," he notes.

Once he made up his mind, he and his assistant Carole set up a small office in a Saint Louis suburban business district. That became the headquarters for Des Lee's philanthropic endeavors. Nothing fancy – certainly not the trappings of executive grandeur. On the walls are family photographs, pictures, and paintings of trains, as well as plaques, citations and awards. On the wall behind his desk is a memento of the past, a large wire collage of the earliest Lee/Rowan wire products that was presented to him on his 70th birthday. At the bottom are the initials, CSWB.

"That was on my license plate. One Sunday, as we were leaving church, the minister asked me what it stood for, and I answered, 'Chicken s….wire bender.' My wife wasn't very pleased and let me know about it when we got home," he said. The letters are no longer on his automobile license. Although he rarely uses this four-letter word or any other in his conversation, they remain on the wall.

So in this humble office environment, Des launched his new endeavor with the same dedication, vision, and energy he had when he started Lee/Rowan. During his first year of retirement, he established the E. Desmond Lee Foundation.

But before he could get too involved with his new venture, his work was interrupted by open-heart surgery – a six-way bypass. "I said if I ever get back to where I feel good again, I want to do something worthwhile. That's another reason I am dedicated to doing what I am doing," he explains.

What Des is doing for the community is one of the most amazing stories of individual charitable generosity in American philanthropy. His philosophy is simple: To encourage and inspire collaboration and partnerships that can produce a synergy that far exceeds the efforts of any one segment working independently. Patterned after the teamwork concept upon which he built his successful company, Des brings together Saint Louis' educational, cultural and social service organizations in partnerships that will have an impact on people in perpetuity. To the best of his knowledge, there is no other program in the country designed to facilitate such collaboration and he is hopeful his idea will spread.

"A scholar once stated that an effective community is where members know what is going on and take responsibility for it," he says. And Des is taking responsibility like no one else. He believes that if Saint Louis is going to prosper in the rapidly changing world, the city must be positioned to embrace change and make the best use of residents' vision, talent, and resources.

When Des sat at the helm of Lee/Rowan he was a hands-on manager. He wanted to know what was going on at all levels of the organization. The same is true in his second venture. Des isn't interested in sitting behind a desk and writing checks. He wants to be involved and be the impetus for opening dialog among the various aspects of the community.

"It's no thrill just writing checks. Anybody can do that. The thrill is in feeling that you've accomplished something and made a change. Most of the things I give to I'm actually involved in," he notes.

It's really about networking, according to Des. "That's all I do. I network and bring people together."

And he is masterful at it. He immediately befriends everyone he meets and puts them at ease with a strong handshake, a warm grin, and a "How the hell are you?" In fact, chances are he'll know a lot about you and your interests within minutes of making your acquaintance.

"Everyone has his or her own agenda, but good things come from organizations working together to make all of them stronger and make all of them more important to the community. Whatever problems we are confronted with, we must feel that we are all part of a team," he said.

"It's amazing the people I've met and things I've gotten to do with Des," notes Carole Ritter. Des includes Carole in every meeting and aspect of this new endeavor. He particularly relies upon her valuable feedback.

"We don't always agree; sometimes he listens, and sometimes he doesn't," she says.

Requests for financial assistance arrive in the mail nearly every day. Because Des is a successful businessman, he understands the importance of staying focused on his mission and reluctantly although frequently has to say no. "We try not to offend anyone, but there is only so much money to go around. I certainly wish I could stretch my money," Des explains.

Many of the requests come from situations of personal tragedy. While Des sympathizes, he doesn't get involved. Others border on the humorous. Carole remembers a request to fund an ostrich farm and another one from a lady who had written a book about lizards. "She wanted him to pop for a video on training lizards," she exclaimed.

Many people ask Des why he is doing this. "Why? Because I want to make Saint Louis a better place to live and work in, and particularly to touch the lives of underserved young people, since the young people of today will assume the role of leaders. The future rests with them."

MAKING THE COMMUNITY A BETTER PLACE

Des Lee calls his philanthropy an "exciting journey of hope."

"But our journey," he says, "will never reach the final destination of having been accomplished. The doing is everything. The having done is nothing."

The first major gift for his pioneering journey was to three major Saint Louis institutions – the Saint Louis Science Center, the Missouri Botanical Garden and the Saint Louis Zoo. While the donation, in and of itself, was substantial, the story behind the contribution is what truly makes it memorable.

Determined to learn how his money would be spent, Des made a call to Dr. Dennis

Wint, then president and CEO of the science center. He inquired as to how a $250 thousand donation would be utilized by the organization. Dr. Wint explained that the money would fund educational programs for children.

A few weeks later, Des had lunch with Peter Raven, the director of the Missouri Botanical Garden. The garden had lost a bond issue election that would have created a taxing district to provide funding. Looking over the material the garden had prepared in anticipation of the additional tax funding, he repeated the same $250,000 offer he had made to Wint as well as the question: what would Raven do with the funds? Of course, Raven discussed programs benefiting children.

After some conversation, Des proposed that instead of giving $250,000 independently to the science center, the garden, and the zoo, he would give $2 million to be divided among the three organizations. He then excused himself and went to the men's room.

Somehow during the walk back from the restroom, he changed his mind again. When he returned he said, "Raven, if I were to give you $2.5 million to be divided among the garden, the zoo and the science center, could the three of you work together on some more programs?"

The answer was a resounding, "Yes."

"He wanted to know if I wanted to go back to the bathroom and think about it some more," Des adds with a chuckle.

Next, Des called Charles Hoessle, the director of the zoo. Although Hoessle was in an important meeting, when Des explained he wanted to give the zoo some money, Hoessle was quickly interrupted. He asked Hoessle the same question and got the same answer. "Of course, they could all work together."

Then Des, being the irrepressible prankster called Dennis Wint again and said, "Dennis, you know that $250,000 I was going to give the science center? Well, I'm not going to do it."

"Dennis probably had a heart attack," Carole said.

But he most certainly recovered quickly when he heard Des' next words. "No, I'm giving you more – $2.5 million to be divided among you. That comes to about $833,000 over five years."

Ultimately the gift was used to undertake a pilot program in science education in one of the low-income school districts. That curriculum spun off into science programs that have trained thousands of students and teachers in the Saint Louis public schools.

"These institutions have a common thread of a scientific approach to learning, and inner-city kids are starved for it," says Des. "Science is a process of thinking, realizing, analyzing, questioning, and searching for meaning. Learning this way builds self-esteem and self-respect."

Later, Peter Raven was quoted as saying, "Des Lee is extraordinarily generous, not just with money but with his time and enthusiasm. His commitment to accomplishing meaningful change in our society is a splendid example to all of us."

In part fueled by the passion his parents had for education, Des focuses much of his energy and money on helping children learn. Education is the key to life success, he believes.

"However I can contribute to the educational process to help those with less education take advantage of the opportunities our modern world has to offer, then I think I am doing a good thing. As long as I can do that unselfishly, that's as good a use of time as I can give to make a difference," he says.

In Des' well-planned but creative philanthropy, he envisions what a gift might do to help people and subsequently outlines specific programs and projects to the recipients. He makes philanthropic decisions as carefully as when he was a businessman, considering the purchase of another company or marketing a new product. He sends his dollars into the community only after he has assured himself that through the institutions on the receiving end, Saint Louis will be a better place to live, and individuals helped by those institutions will find a better life.

The ideas spring from many sources – a chance conversation, an item in the newspaper, a long-held dream, a memory of a past experience. No one, not his family, not Carole, not even he, can predict his next benefactor. He has been known to walk through the door of his office, talking to himself about an idea that has just come to him and set it in motion before he reaches his desk.

Although, his assistant Carole says if he walks in the office and says he's given away another half-million dollars, "I'm going to push him out the door."

"I am a doer, a man of action. That is one of my faults," Des says. "I want to do things right away, and sometimes it's premature. When I propose something, sometimes people will tell me to slow down. My ideas aren't always perfect, but I move and deal with the subject as it unfolds.

"Ideas are not always crystallized. They are usually in a formative stage, and they can be revised with every speck of news that comes out, with every event.

"An idea doesn't come full blown. I think about it day and night. But you have to learn when to drop it. Just like in the business world, a lot of ventures in life don't work out, but you can't let that discourage you. I think a lot of people are frightened by failures but, fortunately, I can take a certain amount of defeat and step up to the plate again."

"Des made up his mind he wanted to donate a significant amount of dollars to the Saint Louis community," explains Des' longtime financial manager Steve Finerty. "He had the motivation to do that. No one pushed him to do it."

While Des is a risk taker, he is not a gambler. Just as he has built his private investment portfolio on what he believes are sound choices, he makes his charitable gifts on the faith that they will pay off in community betterment and human opportunity.

Des has made many single gifts and contributed to literally dozens of fund drives. Recipients include: Springboard to Learning, Herbert Hoover Boys' and Girls' Club, Paraquad, the United Way, the Magic House, the Butterfly House, Ronald McDonald House and a range of large institutions to small agencies. Many are one-time gifts. In other cases, he may continue his contributions to a recipient over months or even years as specific needs arise or as he comes up with an idea for a new program to help the community. His gifts reflect the astonishing range of his interests.

For example, other than playing the drums, Des confesses he has very little musical talent. Jokingly, he says he doesn't know the difference between a harmonica and a piccolo. "Yet I was an enthusiastic drummer in my childhood, and I recognize how much culture enriches the life of this city at every level of study and performance," Des says.

It is that appreciation for music that brought Des to the Saint Louis Symphony. It has become one of his major philanthropies. He is a member of its "big board" and annually contributes generously to its fund drives. But even here he's selective and, like many other of his philanthropies, it sometimes happens seemingly by chance.

One Sunday morning at Ladue Chapel, as the congregation was singing a hymn, he was impressed by the sound of a voice in the pew behind him. After the service he turned around to compliment the singer, who introduced himself as Dick Hoffert, then director of development of the symphony. Des said he would like to do something for the orchestra.

Well, it wasn't long before he heard back. His first thought to help the financially strapped symphony was to launch a major capital fund drive. "There were more than $1 billion in capital fund drives planned by boards at the time, and I realized that to request such large gifts would be extremely difficult. I finally came to the conclusion that the best thing for me to do would be to provide for the retirement of perhaps half of the $2 million debt owed to the State of Missouri. Upon further consideration, I decided that if I was going to make a real difference and set the stage for success, I should volunteer to retire the entire debt of $2 million using a charitable remainder trust," Des recalls. "Bruce Coppock stood up and said, 'This is it! It's time to secure the symphony's future, and your gift will be the catalyst!'"

Retirement of the $2 million debt the symphony owed the state meant the $47 thousand in interest being paid every year could be used to balance the budget.

"Why did I offer this gift?" Des asked. "First, I have thoroughly enjoyed my association with the symphony. Secondly, as a concerned citizen of Saint Louis, I believe that the symphony is a major partner in the life and culture of this great community and I want to be a part of securing its future. And thirdly, the orchestra is one of the greatest in the United States, and this demands support and sound long-range planning to ensure its perpetuation as a leading orchestra with an international reputation."

Then, Des provided the major funding of $750 thousand for the new Saint Louis Symphony Community Music School. It provides an opportunity for talented children at all economic levels to receive superior musical training – much of it by symphony musicians. The school's auditorium now bears his name.

When the symphony needed additional money, he challenged its officials to raise $1 million a year for the next five years and promised, in return, an annual gift of $100 thousand for the rest of his life.

Walking through Powell Hall, the home of the Saint Louis Symphony, he noticed the equipment for the sound system, which an official said was old and needed to be replaced. With a gift of $200 thousand, Des took care of that.

On another day he was touring the Music School – he enjoys seeing how his money is being spent – and noticed the old piano used for student recitals and practice. Shirley Bartzen, director of the music school, agreed that the piano had just about outgrown its usefulness.

"Well Shirley," said the practical Des, "why don't you just get a new one?"

"Des," she answered, "do you know how much a grand piano costs? At least $35 thousand."

The man of action didn't flinch. When he picked up the conversation later with Dick Hoffert, director of development, he offered to write a check and order the instrument.

"No, Des," said Dick, "that's not the way it works." A buyer, he was told, has to consider the size of the instrument, the wood, the wiring, the way it sounds. One doesn't just order a grand piano. It would have to be checked out at the factory.

No problem. A few weeks later after an extended visit to the Steinway factory, Des, his wife, Mary Ann, Carole, then-maestro of the symphony Leonard Slatkin, pianist John Browning, and a young saleswoman were standing in the Steinway sales room in New York. Slatkin and Browning played several of the grand pianos, then agreed on what they considered the best of the group. The price tag for their choice was something over $60 thousand. Des suggested he write out a check for $60 thousand and call it a deal.

"Would you like to take two?" the young saleswoman asked. Mary Ann and Carole almost exploded with laughter as Des said, no, just one would do.

"I am not a musician and don't attend many concerts," he said, "but all major cultural organizations in Saint Louis have formed a pattern that makes the Saint Louis community what it is. Without that, we would be so much poorer. If you are going to take advantage of the wonderful things man has done, the arts are a major part. They enrich the soul," Des says.

Des has also made major gifts to the YMCA and the Herbert Hoover Boys' and Girls' Club. Another major gift endowed the Youth United Way, which established student

United Way agencies throughout the Saint Louis city schools. The students visit the chapters, raise money, and allocate the funds as the parent United Way does. This is unique to the Saint Louis area and educates the students in philanthropy.

Because of his love of trains, Des built an engine, which he donated to the Mercantile Library at UM-St. Louis. Another of his gifts will bring exhibitions such as Monet and Van Gogh to the Saint Louis Art Museum and make it possible for thousands of school children to see them for free.

He even provides the means to the method. Des has helped to provide community organizations with buses to pick up kids from city schools to transport them to area cultural institutions.

His contributions to music and science education programs were not only innovative for Saint Louis children, they also were forerunners of even more ambitious projects in what would become the most celebrated and nationally recognized program in Des Lee's philanthropy.

Des visiting a Grade School Science Education class in Wellston, Missouri

Des Lee donning his Engineer Attire

CHAPTER NINE

THE COLLABORATIVE VISION

"You never own something until you give it away."
                                        – Aaron Hotchner, playwright.

THE VISION – NEVER A FOLLOWER, ALWAYS A LEADER

As is typical of most great leaders, Des Lee was never willing to accept the status quo. He believed there was always room for improvement – to be a better person, to enhance his athletic abilities, to build a better product or to provide better service to his customers. As he embarked upon his second career, he applied these same principles. While he had a desire to make a difference and do something good for the community, he approached his mission with a curious eye and a challenging question of how things could be done better.

The answer came during a chance conversation with Kathy Osborn, former vice chancellor of university relations at the University of Missouri-Saint Louis. She happened to mention that the university had a partnership agreement with the Missouri Botanical Garden and had considered similar arrangements with other educational and cultural institutions.

The light bulb went off in Des' head. It was exactly what he was looking for – teamwork. Next, he talked with then-UM-St. Louis Chancellor Blanche M. Touhill, who is also a visionary, and the two innovators began to plot and plan.

Dr. Touhill told Des about the availability of the Missouri Endowed Professorship Program, a matching grant program for professors through the Missouri Legislature. The legislation provided that private and public resources would be combined to create endowed professorships in perpetuity within the University of Missouri system. Under the plan, each professorship required three sources of funding: a minimum private gift of $550 thousand, a match from the state, and a funded position from the participating institution. (This legislation ceased to exist after 1999.) For its part, the university brought a tenured professor into the faculty – one not already in the university system – and provided the needed facilities and benefits.

In 1996, Des Lee announced the formation of the Des Lee Collaborative Vision: Connecting Saint Louis through Educational & Community Partnerships at UM-St. Louis. The DLCV is an incredible linking of key institutions in the Saint Louis community underwritten by the philanthropy of Des Lee. The unique plan calls for providing endowed professors in perpetuity to serve not only young collegians, but the entire community, with a special emphasis on increasing opportunities for the underserved. Des' initial contribution of $2.75 million for five new professorships and a gift of $550 thousand for a sixth from his friend William R. Orthwein, Jr. was described as "historic in its success in bringing together key Saint Louis educational and cultural institutions to establish programs and share resources that will benefit the Saint Louis community, particularly those individuals who have been traditionally underserved."

"Our strength emanates from sharing a close relationship with our collaborators as we work together to affect the lives of those we touch. I firmly believe that education is the source of all our progress and hope. Universities are one of the best resources for new ideas and creative thinking," Des said.

All the professorships of the Des Lee Collaborative Vision have two overriding conditions: That the professors' work be collaborative in nature; and that they help the region's residents.

"There is a synergy that develops when people work together rather than people working independently and competitively," Des explains. "What I want to do is break down walls that have existed for years in the community between various organizations."

Des' idea of endowed professorships in perpetuity, which is shared by the universities and appropriate community institutions, is believed to be unique in the nation and has become a national model for twenty-first century education.

"I know of no other area in the nation that has developed such a program involving cultural and educational institutions," said Dr. Touhill. "I believe this will be viewed as a national model for collaboration."

"I have never seen anything like it. It is a great model," says Marvin Berkowitz, a former professor at Marquette University and now the Sanford N. McDonnell endowed professor in character education. "A friend of mine is the CEO of a company in Milwaukee, and he has an interest in doing something like this on a smaller scale. I brought him down here to meet Des and to see the model. He was impressed and plans to try to replicate it on a smaller scale."

"Our common goal," Des explains, "must be the education and enlightenment of our children and the development of social consciousness to match. My vision is to build a highway to the underserved."

Although the Collaborative Vision is truly an innovative program, it is in many respects the natural progeny of some of Des' earlier contributions. In 1986, well before he sold the company, Des announced an endowment to be given over five years to Columbia College in memory of his father, Edgar D. Lee. The elder Lee had made a significant mark on Des' life. "It is easy to see how my ideas were shaped by my father," he said.

The guiding principles of the Collaborative Vision read very much like the guiding principles of the Lee/Rowan Company. They are: To collaborate and leverage resources wherever possible; encourage collaboration between all action teams; recognize that collaboration can be challenging; reward innovation and collaboration; respect unique perspectives of all members and groups; keep structure simple and non-bureaucratic; and foster a spirit of mutual understanding, giving, caring, tolerance, unselfishness and hope, with special focus to be given to underserved persons.

"Through the professorships, UM-St Louis will be able to recruit additional distinguished faculty to the campus, students will have greater access to resources at the region's largest cultural institutions, and cultural institutions will now have access to world class teaching and research at the university," said Richard C.D. Fleming, President and Chief Executive Officer of the Saint Louis Regional Chamber and Growth Association.

THE LEADERS OF TOMORROW

Des is a lifelong learner and a proponent of the value of education – a principle instilled in him by his parents. As a leader, he recognizes the importance of ensuring that future generations have the education they need to become the leaders of tomorrow. While education is an integral component of the Collaborative Vision, it pushes far beyond conventional classroom book learning. The Collaborative Vision actually ties the universities to the community's troubles. The mission of the DLCV states: By working together, the region's educational, civic, cultural, business and governmental organizations can offer better opportunities to all citizens…particularly to our underserved populations.

THE E. DESMOND LEE ENDOWED PROFESSORSHIP IN BOTANICAL STUDIES

This position was established as a partnership between the University of Missouri-Saint Louis and the Missouri Botanical Garden to address issues in conservation biology. These two world-class institutions are collaborating in the field of plant molecular systematics, an emerging discipline that utilizes molecular techniques to evaluate evolutionary relationships among species. Not only do these techniques enhance the ability to identify species, but when combined with more traditional approaches, they also permit an understanding of how species are related to each other. Plant molecular systematics also plays a vital role in identifying species of high medicinal, agricultural, and ecological worth.

In addition to the local research projects, leading scientists from around the world are invited to the Saint Louis area to discuss their research and interact with students and faculty at the university and the botanical garden. There is also a biannual public lecture and reception featuring a noted scientific leader in the field of plant systematics.

Dr. Elizabeth Kellogg was named to this endowed chair in August 1998. Kellogg came to UM-St. Louis from Harvard, where she had been an associate professor of biology in the department of organismic and evolutionary biology. She is an expert on various species of grasses and phylogenetics, and she is on the editorial board of the International Journal of Plant Sciences.

E. DESMOND LEE ENDOWED PROFESSORSHIP IN MUSEUM AND COMMUNITY HISTORY STUDIES

Established in partnership with the Missouri Historical Society, its purpose is to "prepare citizens for leadership roles linking historical, cultural and artistic analysis to the discussion of the programs and challenges that face Saint Louisans, Missourians, Americans and the world."

Its goals include education for partnership networking within and among institutions as a necessary means of integrating the diverse issues, specialties and technologies that define educational products and outcomes in the global information age. It also aims to use Saint Louis institutions and Saint Louis area history and culture to develop a national model of museum philosophy, education and practice.

In response to the establishment of the endowed professorship, Dr. Robert Archibald, director of the Missouri Historical Society, said, "Through Des Lee's farsightedness and generosity, our unique community-focused mission can be transmitted around the United States and the world. Students trained through this program will work in institutions that, like the Missouri Historical Society, assist communities in using history – a discussion of who we are – to create broader agreement on our shared values and a common agenda for the future. We hope it will serve as a national model."

The endowed professor Dr. Jay Rounds serves as a faculty member in the anthropology, art and art history departments at UM-St. Louis. He performs research and oversees an outreach program aimed at education of underserved populations locally, nationally and internationally.

"The core of my community service, of course, consists of training students in community-oriented museology, thus providing area museums with highly qualified staff who approach their work with a community perspective," explains Dr. Rounds.

Students have been placed at the following museums in the Saint Louis region: The Missouri Historical Society, Washington Historical Society, Campbell House, DeMenil

House, Eugene Field House, Saint Louis Science Center, Saint Louis Art Museum, Saint Louis Zoo, Faust Historical Park, Whitehaven and the Museum of Transportation.

"Two students are presently working with inner-city youth in the Saint Louis Science Center's Community Science program. They train African-American high school students how to present a science program and then supervise those high-school students in presenting the program to children in inner-city elementary schools," Dr. Rounds said.

E. DESMOND LEE ENDOWED PROFESSORSHIP IN ZOOLOGICAL STUDIES

This professorship was designed to foster a connection between the UM-St. Louis' Department of Biology and the Saint Louis Zoo. "The two institutions had interacted previously on individual graduate student projects. However, no joint programmatic effort had arisen," explains Dr. Patricia G. Parker, who was awarded the professorship in 2000. "The two institutions' overlapping mission to contribute to wildlife conservation provides a natural framework for such a collaboration. These growing efforts will take the sets of special expertise that exist in Saint Louis and apply them to urgent conservation problems elsewhere on earth in some of the world's most illustrious natural sites."

"As partners in this endeavor," said Charles Hoessel, who was the director of the zoo at the time this position was created, "we hope to better understand the natural and human-caused threats facing animal populations in today's world. In the future, preserving the world's diversity and quality human experience will require tremendous collaborative efforts by field biologists, university academicians, zoo investigators, government agencies and interested individuals working together. We are entering a new era of cooperation."

Dr. Parker is a professor at UM-St. Louis and a scientist-in-residence at the Saint Louis Zoo. After she was appointed to the professorship, she worked to identify projects or programs that could contribute to this area of overlapping interests. During the first year of this collaboration, two very different sets of activities began to forge bonds between the two institutions.

Along with her research assistants, Dr. Parker works with experimental laboratory populations, captive zoo populations and natural wild populations of organisms ranging from arthropods (spiders and beetles) to vertebrates (reptiles, mammals and, mostly, birds). They apply a variety of techniques to approach these problems, including behavioral observation and analysis, demographic analyses of populations and the application of molecular markets to understand patterns of genetic relationships among individuals and populations.

A primary research effort is focused on the Galapagos Islands, 600 miles west of South America, straddling the equator. Because the islands were never connected to the mainland, but were born, instead, through volcanic eruptions from the ocean floor, the wildlife that exists there are descendants of the rare colonists that were able to make it that far and survive.

"On this relatively pristine island, the mosquito vector for avian malaria has recently arrived and symptoms of avian pox have been seen on domestic chickens and some of the endemic birds," Parker says. "There is a great sense of frustration and uncertainty regarding the presence and prevalence of these diseases."

Dr. Parker and her graduate students have conducted research on the islands' endemic birds for several years, and so the opportunity to involve the Saint Louis Zoo and UM-St. Louis to contribute to the new animal health concerns was a perfect fit for the Des Lee Collaborative Vision. Through their research, some progress is being made to help understand the disease status.

"In terms of making a contribution to a conservation priority area in need of expert assistance, we could not have begun this initiative at a more appropriate time," states Parker.

E. Desmond Lee & Family Fund Endowed Professorship in Music Education

This professorship was established in partnership with the Saint Louis Symphony Orchestra and Opera Theatre of Saint Louis, but also includes Young Audiences of Saint Louis, Saint Louis Art Museum and many other fine arts organizations in the region. The program is designed to provide an in-depth introduction to opera and its relationship to history, literature and other fields. It also gives students the chance to create their own operas have them performed before family and other students.

Bruce Coppock, former executive director of the Saint Louis Symphony, said, "The creation of this professorship draws the symphony even closer to the University of Missouri-Saint Louis and the Opera Theatre. Bringing symphony musicians and performers from Opera Theatre closer together with professional educators and music education students is nothing short of miraculous."

Distinguished music educator Dr. Douglas L. Turpin was appointed to the professorship in January 1996. He explains, "This program is about making music, listening to music and talking about music."

Because of this endowed professorship, university faculty and symphony personnel are able to provide enriching music education experiences, (called in-services), in Saint Louis city and county public and private schools. Turpin and his collaborative have performed over 834 in-services, reaching thousands and thousands of children in the Saint Louis region.

"Professional musicians and university faculty go into the schools and work directly with the students on the development of musical skills, knowledge and dispositions," Dr. Turpin said. "We are able to have a positive influence on children and the study of music, particularly classical music. They can ask questions of the professional musicians."

Additionally, students and teachers are afforded the opportunity to attend concerts and tour the Saint Louis Art Museum. Approximately, 18,000 free tickets have been distributed to children who might not have the means to purchase them – children who qualify for the reduced or free lunch program.

"One of the best parts is to watch their reaction the first time they walk into Powell Hall (the home of the Saint Louis Symphony). You can see an expression of amazement as you watch them look around," Dr. Turpin said.

As of this writing, the consortium serves 13 school districts and 99 schools where more than 42 percent of the students qualify for free federally subsidized meals. There are approximately 93,423 students attending the Des Lee schools. Of those students, 1.1 percent are Asian, 56.4 percent are black, 0.8 percent are Hispanic and 42.7 percent are white. This is in keeping with Des' vision of serving an ethnically and culturally diverse population.

Because of the structure of the program, many of the same students are involved for several years. Dr. Turpin is quick to note that no one involved in the collaboration tries to overtake any existing institutional strategies. "Our program focuses on the children, not on administrators, or organizations, documents or theory. It's supplement to the local music program," Dr. Turpin explains.

Collaborations have been established with the following organizations in the Saint Louis area: Young Audiences of Saint Louis; Opera Theatre of Saint Louis, Saint Louis Symphony Orchestra; Jazz at the Bistro; Saint Louis Art Museum; and Children's Choir at the Sheldon. "Generally, I love partnerships because they bring together greater resources," says Dr. Turpin.

He is proud of his work in the collaboration and considers Des Lee one of the most unique people he has ever met. "He is a down-to-earth human being, but he has a strong need to give back."

E. Desmond Lee Foundation Endowed Professorship in Art Education

Established in partnership with the Saint Louis Art Museum, the professorship is dedicated to enriching the cultural life of greater Saint Louis by fostering meaningful, educational experiences with the visual arts. Emphasis is placed on programs that feature world-class special exhibitions, permanent collections of the art museum, and benefits to kindergarten through 12th grade students and underserved youth.

"When people ask me about the nature of the Des Lee Professorship in Art Education, I like to tell them that the chief responsibility of the position is to function as a human bridge. Although bridges occasionally may be admired for their cleverness of design, their essential significance resides in the extent to which they connect worthwhile destinations," says Dr. Louis Lankford.

Dr. Lankford was appointed endowed professor in 1997. He came to Saint Louis from Ohio State University, where he had been in the Art Education Department for several years. The professor has a joint appointment at UM-St. Louis in the Department of Art History and the College of Education, serves on the educational staff of the art museum, and directs a program to enrich the work of teachers and students in secondary and elementary grades.

"Teachers are eager to apply what they have learned. Because fine arts teachers, particularly in elementary schools, are responsible for teaching all of the students at their respective schools, it is not uncommon for one art teacher to touch the lives of four hundred or more children on a weekly basis. In one collaborative workshop at the art museum, we reached 50 fine arts teachers, and through them over 10,000 students," Dr. Lankford explains.

Additionally, each year the art museum makes 10,000 tickets available annually in special exhibits to targeted schools and organizations that serve underserved individuals. Half-price tickets are also available to all students to these special exhibits.

"In many respects, art saves lives; it saves lives from meaninglessness, from lifelessness, from drudgery, from being emotionally and spiritually empty, lost or uncentered. Art adds meaning to life, and thoughtfulness, balance, and vigor to individuals and society. Moreover, when we celebrate the arts through history and across cultures, we help to erase destructive prejudices associated with gender, race, ethnicity and preferences. The reality of this power and passion is evident not only in times of crisis, but in everyday life," notes Dr. Lankford.

The arts have the potential to challenge our thinking, show us different ways of seeing the world and reflect our extraordinary diversity. The E. Desmond Lee Foundation Endowed Professorship in Art Education guarantees that all segments of the Saint Louis community will have the opportunity to experience and appreciate world-class art.

"What is rewarding to me is witnessing the emergence of one new artist, one new scholar, one individual discovering extraordinary new personal abilities through his or her encounters with the world of art," Dr. Lankford says. "I have seen the future of the art world pass through my UM-St. Louis office doorway in the form of art and art history students, museum interns and research associates. That's why I feel confident that the power and passion of art will not only be sustained into the next generation, but will climb to new heights. If any of my work has served to nurture and encourage these budding professionals, then my time as a Des Lee professor has been well spent."

WILLIAM R. ORTHWEIN JR. ENDOWED PROFESSORSHIP IN LIFE-LONG LEARNING IN THE SCIENCES

With the ever-changing face of science and technology, more adults than ever will want and need to stay knowledgeable on current advances. The William R. Orthwein, Jr. Life-Long Learning in the Sciences Professorship provides opportunities for adults to increase and update their knowledge of science and technology.

The program includes courses and workshops for teachers, opportunities for adults, particularly retirees, to become current in the sciences; opportunities for retired scientists who have focused on one discipline to become updated in other areas of science and the sponsorship of a public lecture and reception featuring a noted speaker on scientific and technology change involving animals.

"Age is not a barrier to learning," said Dr. Patricia Simmons, who as an endowed professor, holds a joint appointment with the College of Education and the College of Arts and Sciences and serves as a member of the educational staff of the Saint Louis Science Center.

Along with her work with teachers who bring their classes to the science center, Dr. Simmons has created GEAR-UP, Inc. (Gaining Early Awareness and Readiness for Undergraduate Programs). The effort is described as a "collaboration among stakeholders in the education of urban youth to create and sustain a culture of achievement and higher expectations that empowers urban youth and their families to take full advantage of higher educational opportunities."

Implementing the "collaboration" theme of Des' philanthropy, she has organized a GEAR-UP partnership that includes Better Family Life, Harris-Stowe State College, Normandy Public Schools, Maplewood-Richmond Heights School District, Missouri Student Assistant Resource Services, Saint Louis Community College, Saint Louis Public Schools, Saint Louis Science Center, UM-St. Louis, the Urban League, Webster University and Wellston School District.

The class of 2010 is represented by the 972 students who comprise the Students In-Gear cohort and the 972 families, the teachers, counselors and administrators of the four school districts, and the immediate communities surrounding the schools. Wrap-around services are provided to each student and family by the community-based organizations in equal partnership with academic institutions. Leadership development opportunities for students, family members, teachers and counselors and community members have led to a growing awareness of higher education and potential successful careers by students and their families.

More than 100 community and project members, along with GEAR-UP students, pledged their commitment to the success of the program at a kick-off luncheon.

"Whereas, the strength of our future lies in the success of our youth,

"Whereas, good students of today make strong, productive citizens of tomorrow,

"Whereas, the young people we educate today will tomorrow live and carry on the principles of a free and democratic society,

"Whereas, the education of all our community's children is required for a well-prepared workforce and sound economic future,

"Whereas, access to higher education must be in the realm of possibilities for all students, and

"Whereas, it takes a whole community to create and sustain a culture of achievement and high expectations for all children,

"Now, therefore, let it be known that we, the undersigned, endorse GEAR-UP (Gaining Early Awareness and Readiness for Undergraduate Programs) and pledge our readiness to help GEAR-UP, INC.! – In-Gear for Careers."

E. DESMOND LEE ENDOWED PROFESSORSHIP IN SCIENCE EDUCATION I

"The twenty-first century workforce will demand employees who are highly skilled in the sciences, mathematics and technology. We as a nation cannot afford to lag behind the world in our scientific or technological achievements," Des Lee said as he established the E. Desmond Lee Endowed Professorship in Science Education I.

One of the keys to meeting these challenges is to provide quality science education to K-12 students. The professorship was established in July 1996 to enhance pre-service and in-service educators' teaching skills and their science knowledge. Dr. William Kyle Jr. holds the position at UM-St. Louis. Dr. Kyle works with several local science institutions and school districts developing programs to enhance science education literacy. This agenda includes science education reforms and how they affect teacher education and professional development. He also works with the Institute for Mathematics & Science Education and Learning Technology in the following ways: Teaching science education as part of UM-St. Louis' College of Education degree programs; developing methods and materials for K-12 and college students; researching and disseminating research findings;

delivering the institute's programs; and forging productive partnerships with community institutions.

The institute serves as a collaborative resource for teaching, research and service to enhance the scientific literacy among K-12 students as well as the general population in the Saint Louis metropolitan area. The collaboration between the endowed professor and the institute serves as a model for communities across the nation.

E. Desmond Lee and Family Fund Professorship in Science Education II

Enhancing science education research, teaching and service is the major focus for the E. Desmond Lee & Family Professorship in Science Education II. Dr. James A. Shymansky was appointed to the position at UM-St. Louis in December 1997. He works closely with the director of the institute and the E. Desmond Lee Family Professor in Science Education I to develop and implement a teaching and research program, including community outreach, in science education.

Dr. Shymansky's work enhances the efforts of the institute by providing a science education support system and continuous two-way dialogue for in-service teachers that includes providing an annual ten-day summer workshop for teachers that instructs them in the pedagogy and content of hands-on science education, monthly sessions to address various issues the teachers might have in their science teaching programs, and routine on-site visits to schools to provide individual help for teachers.

During the past several years, Dr. Shymansky has been working on a "Science Co-op" project targeting rural school districts in Missouri and Iowa. He also has created a "Passports to Science" project. The idea behind the project is to work with the Saint Louis Science Center to develop special activity bags that parents can use with their pre-school and primary-grade children to stimulate interest in science.

Through the "Mother Goose Asks Why" project, parents from the Wellston School District were shown how to use some award winning children's books as springboards for doing science and mathematics activities. Three luncheon workshops were conducted,

and parents were given six books and a set of six activity bags containing manipulative materials.

As part of the outreach and teacher support, Dr. Shymansky assists with the development of the Teacher Linking Collaborative program that links practicing or retired scientists with classroom teachers to facilitate hands-on science experiences, explore career opportunities, and develop interface opportunities with students, teachers and the private research sector.

"Urban areas have few creeks to wade into and fewer prairies to wander, their museums often relegated to the annual field trip," Dr. Shymansky observes. "Our teachers are distracted by overpopulated classrooms and pressed to produce top scores for standardized tests. What most are not encouraged to produce are creative souls whose latest discoveries in tempera paint or aluminum foil boats can only be measured in retrospect. The solution is clear: to work together, shoulder to shoulder, to create the time and security for children to wonder. This is the vision of Des Lee and those who are building collaborations among parents, schools and communities."

"Public education must be redefined as public collaboration," Dr. Shymansky says. "It requires the cooperation of the entire community as well as schools and parents to reawaken and preserve the next generation.

"Fortunately, a generous few, like Des Lee, have donated vast amounts of wealth to support poor children. Others give their lives to teaching," Dr. Shymansky continued. "Some gifts may be enormous and others may be more humble; but all, in the eyes of God, are the gestures of giants. And it is on the shoulders of such folk, humble as they are, that we raise our children up above the world of exigencies, of memorization, report cards and job interviews, to continue to nurture their divine habit of mind."

EMERSON ELECTRIC COMPANY ENDOWED PROFESSORSHIP IN TECHNOLOGY AND LEARNING

This professorship was established to serve Ranken Technical College and UM-St. Louis. A joint program between the two is directed at school technology coordinators and specialized courses offered to graduate students. The professor, Dr. Carl Hoagland, develops, teaches, researches, evaluates and updates the UM-St. Louis College of Education and Ranken courses that teach the most effective techniques and advances in technological education.

Soon after accepting the position in 1999, Dr. Hoagland began, along with colleague Dr. Joe Polman, to design and develop the E. Desmond Lee Technology and Learning Center as a site for research and scholarship on technology-supported inquiry learning. They recognized two faculty members could not educate the 500-plus students annually certified and the 1,000-plus graduate students about educational technology, nor could they keep up with the rapid pace of innovations. "From the very beginning we included other university faculty and staff in the planning and implementation of the center. My modus operandi was to make the center a collaborative effort," Dr. Hoagland explains.

Now in full operation, the center exceeds its planned goals. More than 50,000 visitors have walked through the doors demonstrating the success of integrating technology into the college curriculum.

One of the center's programs is the Urban Achievement Alliance. Its mission is to look for and support practices and policies that lead to improvements in urban schools. Current activities include a small grants initiative for classrooms – Best Practices Initiative – and an urban education policy workgroup. "Our hope is to more strongly connect teaching practices in urban schools with existing research about what works in urban schools. We also hope to strengthen a community of practice among urban school teachers and encourage them to be informed, to do research, to change their practices based on research and share their results with others," Dr. Hoagland said.

Establishing these professorships serves as evidence of Des Lee's hunger to provide learning opportunities for everyone within the Saint Louis community. These positions serve as the collaboration's foundation – the development of a large community outreach program in conjunction with Chancellor Blanche M. Touhill's leadership at UM-St. Louis.

Agreeing wholeheartedly with Dr. Touhill's philosophy that "no university can stand successfully in isolation," and that "it is only through cooperation that institutions can expect to thrive, expect to be relevant to the communities in which they serve," Des found in UM-St. Louis a hospitable home for this philanthropic program – his collaborative vision. But his work was not done. It was only the beginning.

Dr. Blanche Touhill, Dr. Wendell Smith, Dr. Carol Valenta, Steffinie Harting
Dr. Patricia Simmons and Des Lee

Des Lee Receives an Honorary Doctorate from the University of Missouri-St. Louis. Des is pictured with UM-St. Louis Chancellor Emeritus Blanche M. Touhill and former KMOV-TV news anchor Julius Hunter

CHAPTER TEN

BUILDING ON SUCCESS

"Connecting Saint Louis through Educational & Community Partnerships."

THE VISION GROWS

Since Des founded the DCLV, he has put up between $550 thousand and $1.5 million each to fund endowed professorships at area colleges. There are a total of 35 endowed professors: 31 at the UM-St. Louis; three at Washington University; one at Webster University; and three are unfilled as of this writing. All are endowed for perpetuity, and all belong to the Des Lee Collaborative Vision. The Lee family has funded 22 of the professorships in the collaboration.

But the lives Des is touching through his philanthropy and the partnerships he has nurtured tell the real success of his vision. Highlighted below are additional endowed professorships and a brief snapshot of their remarkable contributions. His undying commitment to assist and educate children remains a common theme throughout.

THE E. DESMOND LEE FOUNDATION ENDOWED PROFESSORSHIP FOR COLLABORATION IN THE ARTS

Dr. Mark S. Weil, chairman of the Washington University Department of Art History and Architecture in Arts and Sciences and director of the university's Gallery of Art, holds this professorship. Dr. Weil is also the director of the Visual Arts and Design Center, which will link the School of Art, School of Architecture, Department of Art History and Archaeology in Arts and Sciences, Gallery of Art and the Art and Architecture Library.

"When I received the professorship, it did not come with a specific mission. I have always loved collaboration, however. The professorship has given me an opportunity to play an active roll in encouraging others to work with me and each other on collaborative projects," Dr. Weil says.

Weil works closely with his colleagues at the Saint Louis Art Museum, where he serves as a trustee in a teaching and community outreach capacity. In the fall of 2002, Dr. Weil initiated the Teaching Gallery, a gallery dedicated to the use of the collections at the Gallery of Art as a teaching resource. The teaching gallery displays rotate according to curricular needs and faculty requests.

Additionally, the Gallery of Art successfully launched a project to update and modernize the art collections' inventory and to render the collections electronically accessible to the public. It also inaugurated a Contemporary Projects series, which is a series of exhibitions of the work of emerging or overlooked artists to bring cutting-edge contemporary art to the Washington University campus and the Saint Louis community.

"Des Lee is an extraordinarily generous individual whose gifts have been a great boon to those of us who have the honor to hold one of the professorships that carry his name as well as the Saint Louis region as a whole. His gifts have increased the quality of research, education and life for the community and will continue to do so in perpetuity," notes Dr. Weil.

SANFORD N. MCDONNELL ENDOWED PROFESSORSHIP IN CHARACTER EDUCATION

To fully understand the mission of this professorship, one has to first understand the context in which it developed. When Sandy McDonnell retired as CEO of McDonnell-Douglas in 1988, he turned his boundless energy to two of his long-standing passions: Ethics and youth development. He had, for example, initiated a corporation-wide ethics program at McDonnell-Douglas and had served as national chairperson of the Boy Scouts of America. Joining these two interests led him to meet with local school and community leaders to brainstorm how to support schools in promoting ethical development in students. This in turn led to the establishment of the Personal Responsibility Education Program (PREP) at the cooperating school districts of greater Saint Louis. PREP was initially in seven Saint Louis area school districts. Linda McKay was hired to direct PREP, now known as Characterplus and expanded to 33 school districts and over 450 schools in a seven-county region in the Saint Louis area, as well as partnering with numerous other schools throughout Missouri. Character education was spreading widely, but in many places its implementation was shallow. McDonnell and McKay decided they needed to go deeper. To do that, two things were needed: An expert in character education and substantive training in character education for school leaders.

With Des' encouragement and an initial gift of $50,000, McDonnell, gave $500,000 to establish the McDonnell Professorship and the Sanford N. McDonnell Leadership Academy in Character Education in 1998. Dr. Marvin W. Berkowitz was tapped for the position in January 1999.

"As the endowed professor, I am generally charged with promoting quality character education, predominantly in the Saint Louis region, but also nationally and internationally," explains Dr. Berkowitz. "Our goal is to help schools help kids become good people as well as smart people. We want to make sure the social, moral and emotional side of kids is being addressed positively and help schools figure out how to do that better."

Schools are increasingly asked to take on roles that earlier in the twentieth century were typically viewed as solely parental responsibilities. One such area is teaching fundamental values. A consensus is emerging that educators, in concert with parents and communities, can help students learn, identify, internalize and act on positive values. Character education is being integrated into the educator preparation programs of the College of Education at UM-St. Louis.

"Teachers continually lament the poor, if any, character education training they received in college. A national sample of colleges of education supported the fact that there is little such training available. I have attempted to increase the level of character education training and expertise within the curriculum," Dr. Berkowitz said.

Additionally, Dr. Berkowitz established the Leadership Academy to educate principals and other education leaders about character education. The academy also works to promote the practice of basic core values, which include caring, honesty, fairness and respect for self and others.

This is an example, Des said, of how public and private schools and educators can expand their mission to meet the changes that inevitably will challenge America in the twenty first century. "What I am trying to do in my professorships is to give a teacher an opportunity to touch the lives of others, either on or off the campus, and to help meet whatever the human need appears to be."

Dr. Berkowitz is pleased with the success of the program. The number of partnerships with schools has more than tripled since the program began. Additionally, Dr. Berkowitz offers thirty to forty free staff-development seminars in schools throughout the Saint Louis region. Over the course of the year, he personally impacts approximately two thousand educators.

In a less structured fashion, Dr. Berkowitz has helped hundreds of schools throughout the region by providing in-service training; making presentations to students; consulting with local education and health groups to promote character development in children; and serving on local task forces, advisory boards and committees concerned with character education and development.

"We are really ramping up the level of expertise in the educational community, and I love it. I came from the ivory tower – 10 years as a professor of psychology at Marquette University. I didn't know if I'd like this. But I was tired of being theoretical, and I wanted to make a mark. This has given me the opportunity to do that," he explains.

"This nation cannot flourish without citizens of character. Children deserve the opportunity to become the best people they can be. Neither of these goals can be achieved if we do not parent and educate children in accordance with principles of effective quality character education," Dr. Berkowitz adds. "I am forever indebted to Des for this chance to make a significant difference in the world and the schools and children of Saint Louis.".

E. Desmond Lee Endowed Professorship for Community Collaboration at Washington University

This professorship originates from the art department at Washington University. W. Patrick Schuchard, Associate Professor and Area Coordinator for Painting in the School of Art, serves as the endowed professor.

Schuchard was a perfect match for this program because his vision, much like that of Des, takes the study and appreciation of art far beyond palette and paint, classroom and studio. He had an idea to turn an eight-story building built in 1927 and owned by Washington University into an attractive and stimulating place for beginning artists to live and get a foothold in the Saint Louis community. Schuchard was able to convince the university to sell the building for one dollar and allow him to create what is now called University Lofts. David Kiel, curator at the Whitney Museum of American Art in New York described the project as, "the most exciting building of its type in the country that I have seen."

The stunning building, once known as the "Drygoodsman," offers 10 market-rate apartment units and 16 low-income units with studio space for the artists who rent them. In the basement, there is also a space for a guest artist in printmaking. Many of the emerging artists who reside at the University Lofts lovingly call it, "The house that Schuchard built."

"The loft project represented my dream of keeping Saint Louis artists here by establishing a thriving community for them," he said. This project and his professorship also allows Schuchard to pursue his visual artistry and projects in the community.

In addition to the loft apartments, the building is home to the Des Lee Gallery, which has enjoyed tremendous popularity since it opened in January 2000. The gallery has been a showcase for the best national and international artists as well as presenting the top talent in the region and educating hundreds of art students each year. In 2002, the gallery was voted the best gallery space by the Riverfront Times, a Saint Louis publication. The article's author stated, "It's only fitting that his name, Des Lee, adorn such an open, inviting, and attractive space. An opening at the Des Lee Gallery is usually one of the most enjoyable events the local art scene has to offer."

The $5.6 million dollar project required a gut renovation but has been a tremendous asset to the Saint Louis region – preventing a drain on the community's talent. In keeping with his desire not to simply write checks but to actually be involved, Des was part of the effort every step of the way.

Schuchard recalls how he and Des would don hardhats, survey the renovation's progress and eat sandwiches on the construction site – sharing a common vision and a dream. He describes Des as a friend rather than a benefactor.

"I really like him," Schuchard says. "I really enjoy him. He's a real person."

Schuchard's warm feelings toward Des and his wife Mary Ann created a challenge for him when he was commissioned to paint a portrait of the couple for the Blanche M. Touhill Performing Arts Center at the University of Missouri – St. Louis.

"It took several months to complete the project. It was difficult because I know them so well and like them so much," Schuchard notes. I really wanted to make the painting special. I wanted it to be a warm representation of the two."

The painting now hangs in the lobby of the beautiful performance hall.

E. DESMOND LEE ENDOWED PROFESSORSHIP IN YOUTH, CRIME AND VIOLENCE

Turning his attention to young people tempted to join gangs, Des endowed a professorship at UM-St. Louis in youth, crime and violence. This professorship is housed in the department of criminology and criminal justice at UM-St. Louis. It's mission is to work with faculty to research and develop a national program model to reduce youth violence and gang activity, to develop a prevention program, to oversee graduate assistants who will work with at-risk young people and their families, to work with other academic units on the campus and with community agencies, to develop relationships with state officials and police, and to seek funding from government and private sources to support ongoing research.

Explaining his concern about the young people who are tempted to join gangs, Des said, "These gangs are growing. They are in the schools, they are on street corners. These kids are on drugs and alcohol and into violence, and they protect their own turf. There are even gangs of young girls.

"The reasons these young people join gangs are poor economic conditions, a lack of jobs and poor parental guidance, a feeling of insecurity, nothing substantial to do with their time and no one to guide them. They are afraid, so they join the gangs for security.

"If I were a young man from the ghetto and didn't have any more hope than they have, I probably would be a strong gang member. I think about my life as a boy. I knew everyone on the block. In a underserved neighborhood people are afraid of crime, drug sales, and prostitution. We have to keep whittling away at that.

"I am not working to reduce crime but to bring hope and opportunity to these young people before they become hardened criminals. They will continue to be involved in crime and violence unless we provide an alternative. They feel they have no hope of realizing the American Dream."

Dr. Finn Esbensen is the endowed professor for this program and began in August 2001. He sponsors an Annual Youth Violence Prevention Conference each year. The conference is intended to provide attendees with knowledge of successful youth violence prevention strategies in other American cities as well as address the role of guns in youth violence.

Additionally, Dr. Esbensen established a tutoring/mentoring program through the Saint Louis Police Department cadet training program. The police recruits are assigned to elementary schools for the duration of their training and visit their schools each Wednesday. The program has the dual objectives of improving police/community relations and improving student reading abilities.

The E. Desmond Lee Endowed Professorship in Urban Education in Cooperation with the Saint Louis Public Schools

Closely related to the professorship on youth, crime and violence, this endowed chair was established in conjunction with the Saint Louis Public Schools. "We were enthusiastically invited into the public school district by Superintendent Cleveland Hammonds and further endorsed by the Board of Education," Des explained.

Des believes that as a nation, we face an alarming array of human problems created by societal and technological change. All of society's institutions are impacted by rapid change, especially our schools. Today's teachers juggle the challenges of teaching students from disparate educational levels and diverse backgrounds, including many at-risk children whose needs cross discipline and professional boundaries.

Educators and administrators in lower income areas are especially in need of creative solutions to in-service and pre-service teacher education and professional development. A constant stream of new, energetic young teachers with fresh ideas must flow into all schools.

"This will provide a permanent system to infuse Saint Louis public school teachers and administrators with new knowledge, resources, leadership and pride to carry out their important work. It is clear we must create collaborative links within the community to help educators with these complex issues to shine a new light on our children," Des says.

During the past several years, the professorship has produced a number of major initiatives and programs. For example, the Career Transition Certification Program was created to address critical teacher shortages in the Saint Louis schools. The program is designed to prepare mid-career professionals for teacher certification in Missouri. The two-year, immersion model program (educators learn to teach while teaching full-time) is experience-driven and standards-based. The goal is to provide the support, coursework, seminars and professional experiences needed by participants to develop the skills and knowledge necessary to meet the standards for certification established by Missouri. While teacher shortages continue, the number of shortages in critical needs areas such as science and mathematics have been greatly reduced. Furthermore, national averages for retaining new teachers in urban districts are approximately 50 percent. The retention rate of Career Transition teachers is over 80 percent.

Additionally, the Saint Louis Public Schools Professional Development Academy was established following the Board of Education's approval of the professional policy. The PDA has served thousands of teachers, administrators, staff and local educational organizations. The PDA provides meeting space, state-of-the-art technology labs and classrooms for district-wide professional curriculum.

The urban education professorship aims to meet the special needs of urban educators by developing, promoting and fostering pre-service and in-service teacher and administrator education along with professional development. Through the Preparing Urban Leaders for Urban Schools program Saint Louis Public Schools, teachers who aspire to be principals receive leadership training. Participants who complete the two-year program receive a master's degree in education and principal certification. Graduates answer a critical need in the city schools by filling vacancies for principals, assistant principals and literacy coaches.

"This is a major service to the SLPS and the community in a time when there is a shortage of urban trained and certified administrators," said Dr. Lynn Beckwith, Jr., who was appointed interim endowed professor in August 2003.

"Des Lee has met a critical need of UM-St. Louis and the SLPS to provide direct assistance to the largest school district in Missouri at a time when the schools need it most," Dr. Beckwith says. "His sponsorship of this professorship exemplifies that he is a true humanitarian and that UM-St. Louis is, indeed, an urban university and cares about the welfare of the children of Saint Louis through the enhancements provided to its teacher and administrative corps in the area of professional development."

In that same vein, principals working at schools that feed Vashon High School in the inner city can attend an instructional leadership program created in conjunction with this professorship – The Vashon Education Compact Principals Initiative. The Collaborative

Vision has also enabled SLPS administrators to travel to national conferences, and students from four Saint Louis high schools were able to travel to UM-St. Louis to participate in a program that teaches children about voting.

Dr. Beckwith praised Des' commitment to urban education. He particularly noted comments Des made in a UM-St. Louis magazine about developing empathy for the black troops he commanded during World War II. "This was well before the civil rights movement of the 1960s. Therefore, his stance may have been unpopular at that time," Dr. Beckwith says. "As an African-American, his statement made a deep impression on me and helped me to understand the true measure of this man called E. Desmond Lee."

E. DESMOND LEE ENDOWED PROFESSORSHIP IN EDUCATION FOR CHILDREN WITH DISABILITIES IN CONNECTION WITH THE VARIETY CLUB OF GREATER SAINT LOUIS

In 1999, Des was named the Variety Club of Greater Saint Louis' Man of the Year. In response, he paid tribute to the club's long and deep concern for children with disabilities and announced the creation of this endowed professorship.

"In a perfect world, all children would grow up in a nurturing environment, in strong families, in supportive learning situations. They would have hope, dignity and self-esteem. They would have friends. They would have learned how to learn, to accept challenges, and to push themselves to their own limits – whatever they might be," Des said.

"However, the future isn't so clear for an enormous number of children under the chronological age of 21. Many children with disabilities are experiencing little other than frustration and failure within our educational and social systems. The need is escalating to establish a supportive channel for resources, collaborative research and programs for children with disabilities to address their education, socialization and transition to becoming independent and productive members of our community. The professor will teach, do research, establish community outreach programs, promote education and provide services and resources to children and their parents."

Des also noted that the new professorship is close to his heart because of his granddaughter Lyrica, who is an autistic child. Lyrica and her mother Gayle were on hand for the announcement and to share the spotlight with Des' younger daughter, Christy, and his son, Gary.

Gayle read an introduction for Lyrica's response to her grandfather's dedication of the new professorship to her.

Gayle's introduction:

"I am honored to be here with you tonight as a representative of the Lee family to speak on behalf of two of the greatest loves of my life, my father Desi and my daughter Lyrica.

Although to a casual observer, their lives might appear to be vastly different and unrelated, to me, who has been deeply touched by both, I see a common spirit, wisdom, and courage to express their own uniqueness, to share their message of love, to teach, uplift, and inspire eyes to see, ears to hear, minds to understand, and hearts to feel. Their greatness is not in what they have done, but in who they are.

As a tribute to all of us here tonight gathered on behalf of persons not with disabilities, but simply persons with grand and differing abilities, I would like to share the words typed by my daughter, Lyrica, on her computer, a computer that unlocks her silence within and sets free her voice, her lyrics, her music, the song of her soul, the essence of her being."

Lyrica's words:

Love tell my grandpa thanks on jump my life to might place
Must help others to have awesome thing I got
Most noteworthy were my therapies on talking
Very lost on no voice
Best I hear hope
I got hope in learning to read
Gave me jolt I needed to communicate by typing
I found my love in typing my life on autism
Got my fast pace on learning when people treated me like person who gave them tip top heart in my writings

I faced my disability letting my heard have gold on little greatness
No have my voice but I have love on my life
I think that everyone in disability needs hope to find their own greatness
You bring us bits of help in therapies but loads of help when you give us positive look
on top person inside us.
Yell heart is loud in person with disabilities
Tap into our person inside, not our outside place of hurt
You reach our hear, you will help on our hope
Hope is doorway to love
Love is doorway to trying
And trying is doorway to holding on to new life
Therapies and education take openness to receive
Openness comes when you help us kill our sadness
And pain that we are not hip
Once we see our person as gold inside, progress starts
Molts us to butterfly to live in great love on our life.

Dr. Phil Ferguson, who came to Saint Louis from the University of Oregon, has held this endowed professorship since September 2002. Its mission is to work with various agencies and institutions to help the disabled and families of children with disabilities participate as full members of the community.

"Des' daughter Gayle had spent a year before I got here working for the university and surveying the needs of families and students with disabilities. It was a tremendous help," explains Dr. Ferguson.

In addition to his work in the community, Dr. Ferguson is also working with teacher preparation programs in special education at UM-St. Louis to help teachers work with special needs children in the classroom and to include the students' families as well.

"We are also developing a family oral history archive, which will contain experiences of families with children with disabilities. This will provide insight for researchers to get the families' perspective in terms of what's supportive and what is not," he adds.

While Dr. Ferguson admits he wasn't looking to change positions when he came to Saint Louis, he is amazed and very happy.

"It is exciting because I have a lot of freedom, but freedom with certain values and a purpose. It was a natural fit for me because I have a special needs child, and I have always wanted to do something to make a difference," he explains. "Plus, Des is wonderful to work with. He is a real piece of work," Ferguson adds warmly.

THE E. DESMOND LEE ENDOWED PROFESSORSHIP IN TUTORIAL EDUCATION

Income has been shown to have the largest role in predicting a child's level of school success. Chances that a student will fall behind in school increase by two full percentage points for every year the student spends growing up in poverty. These at-risk students represent the largest untapped pool of future job candidates to meet the increasing demand for well-educated minority employees in the Saint Louis region.

Des Lee had a vision that the underserved youth could be supported in their development as future citizens through a collaboration of universities and after-school programs. Acting upon that vision, he created the E. Desmond Lee Regional Institute of Tutorial Education (RITE) and this professorship. The mission of the professorship is to enhance the university's education outreach efforts through a joint program with 10 of the finest youth service and education organizations in the Saint Louis region through the United Way of Greater Saint Louis.

Dr. Judith Cochran was appointed to this endowed professorship in September 1998, having come to Saint Louis from Wright State University in Dayton, Ohio. According to Dr. Cochran the program is designed to work with the staff of each institution to develop and enhance existing tutorial programs based on the special needs of at-risk students, and using College of Education undergraduates and graduates as tutors and interns, to conduct workshops and seminars to educate the staff of the participating institutions on skill progression, curriculum innovation and hands-on learning techniques. The program is also designed to initiate evaluation and research components for assessing the effectiveness of pre-collegiate initiatives, tutoring programs, and seminars and workshops.

"We have worked to create after-school tutoring programs for many local organizations and agencies," Dr. Cochran says. "We tutor children who cannot read textbooks because they read three or four years below their ability level. Some of these students are left alone after school with no one to help them when they get stuck, so these tutoring sessions help these students. Our tutors offer a more one-on-one approach and will take the extra step to help students. They get the student's top focus on study skills. Instead of giving them answers, we encourage them to be more independent."

One of the programs is called Academics to Athletics, and it reaches out to more than 50 kids at an agency called ECHO (Emergency Children's Home). Supported by many local sports teams, the program uses the kids' interest in sports to engage them in reading and math activities that range from computing player and team statistics to reading player biographies to corresponding with players.

"While most of the students who live at ECHO are 12 years old and older, they read and compute math on the fourth-grade level. The children who demonstrate good behavior are brought to the campus to receive tutoring. There is a waiting list of ECHO students who want to participate," Dr. Cochran said.

ECHO children have improved grades in 70 percent of the cases. In a controlled research study, 89 percent of the children who received Academic Athletic tutoring at the Saint Louis Housing Authority improved their reading by at least one grade level. Additionally, 75 individual case studies of participating children showed improvements in reading, math and grades.

"The success of the program can be measured by the academic skill and attitude improvement of participating children. Students from programs like ECHO now walk up the steps of the university and say they are coming to this university when they grow up. The academic development of RITE youths has been much greater than expected by program administrators and participating educators," Dr. Cochran notes.

RITE obtained an $800 thousand grant to improve the academic levels of the struggling Wellston schools in Saint Louis. In the summer of 2003, all of the 150 first through eighth graders enrolled in the summer school at Wellston financed by RITE improved in math and reading.

"This is just one example of the success our many programs have had," Dr. Cochran said.

Other cities and organizations are taking notice too. RITE has received national awards for its work and educational programs across the country are using RITE's programs as models.

One important progeny of this program has been the E. Desmond Lee Regional Library for Tutorial Education. It contains videos, books, and resources for children and tutors. Located on the UM-St. Louis campus, the library also has extensive files and notebooks on best practices for tutoring. These strategies have been obtained from learned society-reviewed materials, Web sites, teaching strategies and conferences. This library is unique in its focus and materials.

"There is nothing like this in the country," explains Dr. Cochran. "After five years, we are definitely having an impact."

THE E. DESMOND LEE ENDOWED PROFESSORSHIP IN EXPERIENTIAL AND FAMILY EDUCATION IN COOPERATION WITH FOREST PARK FOREVER

The year was 1904 and Saint Louis was center stage, as people came from all corners of the world for the greatest exhibition of all time – the 1904 World's Fair in Forest Park. Most of the buildings have come down, but the grandeur of the park remains – a prized possession for the Saint Louis region. Dr. Jim Wilson, outreach and education chief for the Missouri Department of Conservation, joined the Des Lee Collaborative Vision as an endowed professor in November 2002. He sees his mission as developing stewardship for Forest Park through experiential education programs. Dr. Wilson's responsibilities include developing credit and non-credit programs for children and adults using the resources of this cultural and natural gem of Saint Louis.

"Community parks contribute to the quality of life in the community and it is important to help people understand these resources and how they significantly contribute to their lives," Dr. Wilson says.

"I remember the first meeting I had with Des. During our discussion, I mentioned something about a very minor part of the position and shared my thoughts. But he really keyed in on it, and the next time I met with him, he asked me about it. I was very impressed with his desire to have that kind of detailed involvement in the work," Wilson notes.

Like most people, Wilson is struck by Des' sincerity and his outgoing nature. "He has a true sense of commitment and an amazing way of relating to the community. He is forthright and a regular person, but he had the vision and the ability to create this amazing collaboration," Wilson adds.

E. DESMOND LEE ENDOWED PROFESSORSHIP FOR RACIAL AND ETHNIC DIVERSITY AT WASHINGTON UNIVERSITY

With a doctorate in social welfare from the University of Washington in Seattle, Dr. James Herbert Williams came to Saint Louis to teach at Washington University. Subsequently, he received the endowed professorship for racial and ethnic diversity, which was right in line with the focus of his research.

"The first time I met Des, we went to lunch at his private club, and it was like entering the room with a politician. Everyone knew him, and he made sure he stopped to talk to everyone and introduce me. Then, we sat down. He turned to me and said, 'Tell, me what's wrong with the world, and this whole race thing.' I thought, this guy is going to challenge me for years to come," Dr. Williams recalls.

The mission of the professorship is to do community work and research related to addressing issues of race and ethnicity in the Saint Louis area.

"I believe my role is to help raise the awareness and understanding of the issues of race and ethnicity. I don't do race relations research. I do social issues of the underrepresented in our society and try to understand how we can make a change in their lives. Race is an issue, but economics is also an issue and sometimes the terms are used synonymously," Dr. Williams explains.

"This chair and the collaborative allow me to involve myself in the community, working with the school districts and the family courts. It gives me the opportunity to be

involved in diversity dialog in the community. For example, we have been involved in a dialog program for the black and Jewish communities to discuss diversity and tolerance," he said.

Des is truly concerned about the impact of racial and ethnic issues. He is well versed in the topic, as he is in most of the professorship areas he endows; however, put him in a room with all these Ph.D.'s, and you'll find him defaulting to his country-boy charm, often saying, "I'd don't know anything. I'm honored to be here in your presence."

"He said that to me once, and I said, 'Des, let's get real. You couldn't have accomplished all you have accomplished without being a very learned and astute professional," Williams said.

Behind that humble attitude is a brilliant, compassionate man, but as Williams notes, his personality is endearing.

ARONSON ENDOWED PROFESSORSHIP IN MODERN & CONTEMPORARY ART HISTORY IN CONNECTION WITH LAUMEIER SCULPTURE PARK

Glen P. Gentele was appointed the Aronson Endowed Professor in Modern & Contemporary Art History at UM-St. Louis in 2002. The goal of the professorship is to expand public awareness of sculpture and modern and contemporary art. It is also charged with providing outreach and descriptive evidence of the achievements of twentieth and twenty-first century artists. In addition to his educational and community work, Gentele is also the director of the Laumeier Sculpture Park and Museum in Saint Louis. Laumeier is a 98-acre park with a collection of more than 85 sculptures by artists of international acclaim, such as Anthony Caro, Mark di Suvero, Donald Judd, Alexander Liberman, Robert Morris, Michael Heizer, Charles Ginnever, Dennis Oppenheim, George Ricky and the world's largest single collection of Ernest Trova Sculptures. The park is accredited by the American Association of Museums and is an institution of international significance with over 300,000 visitors annually coming to explore, learn and understand the complexity and beauty of monumental works of art.

A summer art camp at the park serves approximately 600 children, and an annual art fair brings about 20,000 visitors and 150 artists/artisans from across the country.

THE TERESA M. FISCHER ENDOWED PROFESSORSHIP FOR CITIZENSHIP EDUCATION

This professorship was established to raise the profile and impact of citizenship education for students from kindergarten through the 12th grade. In addition to teaching, This professor researches citizenship education and publishes his work. He also functions as an academic resource for UM-St. Louis students and faculty as well as serves and developing other citizenship initiatives. This professor has the responsibility for directing the Citizenship Education Clearing House, which provides technical assistance to area school districts on citizenship education. CECH was founded in order to prepare young people for responsible citizenship. In pursuit of this mission, CECH has developed an array of programs that engage Saint Louis area students in the hands-on study of politics and policy.

For example, on November 7, 2000, more than 42,000 Saint Louis area students in grades K-12 went to the polls with their parents and voted for president, U.S. senator, governor, and a host of other federal, state and local officials along with a variety of state and local ballot propositions. A network of nearly 2,000 volunteers, including about 400 high school students, supervised the students' voting on optically scanned ballots at nearly 300 Kids Voting poll sites. When the polls closed, the volunteers collected the students' ballots and delivered them to the computing facilities at the UM-St. Louis, which tabulated the ballots and posted the results on the Kids Voting Missouri Web site on election night.

Another program, CECH-UP, is a major school-based initiative that operates both in the Saint Louis region and across Missouri. Developed by CECH in cooperation with the Saint Louis Area City Managers Association and Urban Extension at UM-St. Louis, the program teaches middle school students about local government in the Saint Louis area and involves them in projects in their own communities.

Ultimately, the success of CECH's programs must be measured in terms of improvements

in the quality of citizenship. Students who participate in CECH programs should know more about the political process than those who don't and, as adults, CECH students should be more likely to vote and participate in other forms of civic engagement.

This position was initially filled in September, 1995 by Dr. Timothy O'Rourke. Subsequently, Dr. O'Rourke assumed a position as Dean at another University. The University of Missouri-St. Louis is searching for a replacement at the time of this writing.

E. DESMOND LEE ENDOWED PROFESSORSHIP IN COMMUNITY COLLABORATION & PUBLIC POLICY

"Livable communities don't just happen. They are created by the people who live in them."
– Des Lee

This professorship is the Director of the Public Policy Research Center (PPRC) and also a part of the Department of History and the Public Policy Administration Program at UM-St. Louis.

The PPRC is committed to improving the development and implementation of public policies that foster livable communities. This commitment involves working in partnership with public, private and non-governmental agencies to develop strategies that promote the economic well-being of citizens, encourage social diversity and plurality of lifestyle, and advance the sustainability of the natural and built environment. The center also works closely with faculty and students from all university colleges and with other centers and institutes.

The PPRC focuses its resources on issues related to neighborhood and community development, economic vitality, governance (at the local, county and regional levels), land-use and transportation policy planning and health, education, and social policy. To accomplish its goals, the center has developed partnerships with local, county, regional and state government organizations and citizens' groups.

"In some small way, I believe the work of improving the region has been advanced," notes past professor Alan Artibise.

EIICHI SHIBUSAWA-SEIGO ARAI ENDOWED PROFESSORSHIP IN JAPANESE STUDIES

In 1999, Mr. Seigo Arai, businessman and friend of the Shibusawa family, made a generous gift to UM-St. Louis to establish the Eiichi Shibusawa-Seigo Arai Professorship in Japanese Studies. The professorship strengthens the faculty and curriculum in East Asian studies by providing enhanced teaching, research and community programs about Japan.

Eiichi Shibusawa's life spanned the most turbulent period in modern Japanese history. With respect for the value of permanence and change, Shibusawa is credited with modernizing the Japanese economy. He was also a strong supporter of improved U.S.-Japan relations. Not only did he recognize that the two countries had much to learn from each other, but he also believed that their prosperity was dependent on the strength of their relationship.

In recognition of the accomplishments of Eiichi Shibusawa, the Center for International Studies named Japanese and international business expert Dr. Allan Bird to serve as the first holder of the endowed professorship. Working with the center, general community and Japanese-Americans, Dr. Bird develops programs for campus and community audiences about Japanese business and the U.S.-Japan relationship. The professor also cooperates with the relevant faculty at UM-St. Louis and Washington University to strengthen multidisciplinary programming about Japan. Dr. Bird collaborates with the other international professors and the center to develop a comprehensive international program highlighting the diversity of Saint Louis' ethnic heritage.

For example, Dr. Bird has hosted the Midwest Japan Seminar. The seminar was an interdisciplinary network of scholars conducting Japan-related research at universities throughout the Midwest. In addition, Dr. Bird, in conjunction with the Center for International Studies, sponsors performances by Japanese artists such as the Tonda Traditional Banraku Puppets and the Shizumi Dance Theatre as part of the center's International Performing Arts Series.

THE HELLENIC GOVERNMENT-KARAKAS FAMILY FOUNDATION ENDOWED PROFESSORSHIP IN GREEK STUDIES

The initiative to create a professorship in Greek studies came from the Greek-American community in Saint Louis. Motivated by a common commitment to preserve the Greek heritage in the United States, 300 individual contributors, the government of Greece and the Karakas Family Foundation pooled their resources to create the Hellenic Government-Karakas Family Foundation Endowed Professorship in Greek Studies at UM-St. Louis.

With the assistance of a community-based advisory committee, the Greek Studies program promotes the study of ancient, Byzantine, and modern Greek culture. In accordance with the wishes of the donors to enhance the preservation of Greek language, history and heritage, this professorship offers courses in modern Greek language and culture. The program is the first of its kind in Missouri.

In addition to the teaching and research components of the Greek studies professorship, the Karakas Family Foundation Alliance for the Advancement of Hellenic Studies has been established to develop and promote outreach education in Greek studies and culture for the broader community. These programmatic activities include lectures, symposia, concerts and a film series. The Alliance annually sponsors a major international conference. According to Nick Karakas, chairman of the Karakas Family Foundation and the Greek Studies Advisory Council, these programs fill an important void in the understanding and appreciating the input of the Hellenic civilization in Western thought. They explore, feature and publicize the rich legacy of Hellenic culture and foster the continued interest and development of Hellenism in the Saint Louis area, the Midwest and the country at large. For students, the Greek studies program creates new opportunities to study another language and culture. Dr. Michael B. Cosmopoulos holds this professorship. He works to internationalize the experiences of the UM-St. Louis students and to provide leadership for Missouri and the Saint Louis region.

Dr. YS Tsiang Endowed Professorship
in Chinese Studies

Moved by the plight of peasants in China, Dr. Yien-Si Tsiang began his life of public service with the study of agriculture. In his policy-making role, Dr. Tsiang was the architect of Taiwan's land reform program, a policy that formed the foundation for the country's economic modernization and remains a model for other developing countries. Throughout his many years of exemplary service to the government and people of Taiwan, Dr. Tsiang distinguished himself as a scholar, researcher, administrator and statesman. The Dr. YS Tsiang professorship in Chinese studies was established in recognition of Dr. Tsiang's outstanding contributions through the generosity of the Chiang Ching-Kuo Foundation for Scholarly Exchange, Far Eastern Textile Ltd., Liu International Foundation, Ministry of Education, Republic of China, Taipei Fortuna Hotel and the United World Chinese Commercial Bank.

By enhancing teaching, research and community programs about China, the professorship builds on the university's strong foundation of expertise in East Asian studies. The selection of Dr. Hung-Gay Fung as the first holder of the professorship reflects the university's recognition of the economic importance of the Asia-Pacific region. Dr. Fung's expertise in international and Chinese business provides an invaluable resource for the campus and community.

The professorship supports conferences, distinguished speakers' programs, visiting scholars, faculty research and cultural programs about China. It not only strengthens the academic excellence of the university, but also brings a global vision to the Saint Louis region and enhances the relationship with the local Chinese-American community.

"My goal is to increase the recognition of UM-St. Louis within Saint Louis' Chinese community and increase the reputation of the university so that the outside world recognizes that we are a key player within China," Dr. Fung says.

To achieve his goals, Dr. Fung has served on a variety of boards in the region including: the Organization of Chinese Americans, the Chinese Language School, the Chinese Culture Day, the Saint Louis Chinese Association and the Mid-West Chinese-

American Science and Technology Association. Dr. Fung has also edited two English-language Chinese journals: China and World Economy and Chinese Economy. He also has organized conferences and seminars with Chinese partners in China and offered a training program to municipal officials in Nanjing.

He feels that his work and Des' go hand in hand in fostering good relations between local and Chinese communities, China and China interests. "Des Lee has great insight that recognizes the importance and vitality of cultural diversity," Dr. Fung says. "I appreciate his contribution to UM-St. Louis in particular and the community in general."

THE JEFFERSON SMURFIT CORPORATION ENDOWED PROFESSORSHIP IN IRISH STUDIES

In 1996, Dr. Michael Smurfit pledged the funds to create the Jefferson Smurfit Corporation Endowed Professorship in Irish Studies. As a major multinational corporation with more than 50,000 employees in 25 countries, Jefferson Smurfit Corporation clearly exemplifies what it means to be a good corporate citizen in the era of global economic interdependence. Integral to the efforts to internationalize UM-St. Louis, this professorship represents another important step in ensuring that students and the community understand and communicate with people of different cultures.

Two professors, Drs. Gearóid Ó hAllmhuráin and Eamonn Wall, provide leadership in the development of Irish studies on the campus. These professors take an interdisciplinary approach to promote teaching, research and community service in the Irish arts, humanities and history. Working with the Center for International Studies, the Irish-American community and the public, the professors develop programs for campus and community audiences about Ireland and the Irish expatriate experience. The professors also collaborate with the other international professors and the center to develop a comprehensive international program.

The establishment of the Jefferson Smurfit Corporation Distinguished Lecturer series has permitted the Center for International Studies to offer outstanding programs for campus and community audiences. Among them has been the week-long visit of Dr. Nicholas Canny, a noted Irish historian from the National University of Ireland who spoke on the colonization of Ireland. In addition, the professorship sponsored the visit of the Honorable John Hume, Nobel Peace Prize laureate who spoke about the peace process in Northern Ireland.

"This collaborative allows us to interface with and learn from Des Lee's philosophy of educational and community development," Dr. Ó hAllmhuráin said. "It gives us a forum to communicate with our colleagues at UM-St. Louis and at other Saint Louis-area universities where Mr. Lee has endowed professorships and to share our own mission of promoting Irish and Irish-American arts, scholarship and culture in the greater Saint Louis community and throughout the midwestern states."

Other activities the professors orchestrate include visiting Irish and Irish-American poets and musicians reading and performing in schools throughout the Saint Louis area. The professors themselves read, perform, direct, and judge various artistic and cultural events at UM-St. Louis. Those events typically attract 2,000 people a year to the campus.

"All our Irish events are open to the public and are well-attended," notes Dr. Wall. "I am encouraged that about 20 percent of our enrollment is garnered from the surrounding community, and this is something I hope to build on for the future."

HUBERT C. MOOG ENDOWED PROFESSORSHIP IN NURSING & HEALTH STUDIES

This professorship was given by Dorothy R. Moog in honor of her husband, Hubert C. Moog, former chairman of Moog Automotive Inc., and was the first established in 1995 under state enabling legislation for such endowed professors. Several leading nursing educators held the position on a visiting basis. The current professor, Dr. Roberta Kari Lee, was appointed in 1997. She brings to the region the most advanced thinking in nursing research, education and practice known to the profession. In the position, Dr. Lee combines the highest quality teaching and scholarship with research and innovation in education. She works with health organizations and recruits scholars from across the nation to educate nursing students.

She particularly emphasizes the research and study of injury prevention and the elimination of violence against women. Dr. Lee also is an expert in youth suicide as well as minorities and youth violence. Her work includes a research project on youth suicide attempts with the Centers for Disease Control and Prevention. She also served as a consultant to the American Association of Suicidology and National Institutes of Justice. She devotes great attention to guiding her graduate nursing students on a variety of public health issues, including an examination into who typically reports child abuse as well as parental supervision and childhood injuries.

While the Moog professorship was created prior to the Collaborative Vision, Dr. Lee said her mission dovetails with those of the university and Des Lee. She is particularly impressed, she said, with Des' active engagement in the work of all the professors in the DLCV.

"He's very keenly interested in everything that the endowed professors are doing," Dr. Lee said. "He is interested in collaboration with the community and the college. He has very broad interests."

E. DESMOND LEE ENDOWED PROFESSORSHIP FOR COMMUNITY COLLEGE TEACHING, ADMINISTRATION AND LEADERSHIP ACADEMY

The next generation of leaders will not come just from the ranks of four-year universities. They will earn their educational stripes at community colleges in Missouri and across the nation – as students as well as educators and administrators. This professorship endeavors to spread the influence of the DLCV throughout the community college system in Missouri and spark improvements in urban and rural areas across the state. It aims to provide professional development opportunities for the policy makers and leaders of the community colleges and to develop strategies to help the community colleges improve student achievement in the primary and secondary school system.

"Increasingly, students in urban and rural areas of Missouri start their higher education in community colleges. Thus, it is vital to have a program that supports and sustains the vision of educating all the children and all of the people," said Dr. Charles McClain, who was appointed on an interim basis to the professorship in August 2003.

Early on, Dr. McClain began developing the vision for the Des Lee Leadership Academy for Community Colleges. It includes working with the state's community colleges and the Presidents' Council of Community Colleges. Dr. McClain has developed a draft plan for the Leadership Academy.

"Fitting a new academy into an organization with a traditional model of course and credit without being constrained by the model requires creative effort, sustained energy and enormous courage. The professorship is to do what is not being done in traditional offerings," Dr. McClain says. "Such work reflects the history and life of the founder, creator and benefactor of the professorship, Mr. Des Lee. Those of us who are blessed to have one of his professorships have directly felt his enormous talent for serving those who need someone to help them see a way out of their condition."

E. DESMOND LEE ENDOWED PROFESSOR FOR AFRICAN/AFRICAN AMERICAN STUDIES

The creation of this professorship came at a particularly auspicious time. As the elements for economic, social, and political renewal and creating changes throughout Africa, the E. Desmond Lee Endowed Professorship in African/African-American Studies supports the work of a distinguished expert in the field of African/African American Studies. Through teaching and research that focus on African and African-diaspora studies, the history, contributions and status of African nations and their descendants are becoming better known. This enhanced knowledge is creating a new appreciation for the cultural heritage of African-Americans in the Saint Louis community and acknowledges their contribution to the unique nature of our local cultural diversity.

Cecil Abrahams, formerly of the University of Western Cape in South Africa, was appointed to fill this position in 2003. He is collaborating with the other international professors and the Center for International Studies to develop a comprehensive international program. He also plays a leadership role in the development of African/

African-American studies at UM-St. Louis as well as creating programs for community audiences about the connection of persons of African heritage to the African continent.

Most importantly, Dr Abrahams is trying to break down the barriers to African-Americans' success in Saint Louis. He uses speakers and experiences from his native South Africa to show how people with fewer opportunities and resources than Saint Louisans are overcoming racism and excelling.

"South Africa is a kind of beacon, and there is much that African-Americans can find some pride in," Dr. Abrahams said.

"African-Americans must emphasize the importance of education within their culture as a force to overcome poverty and racism. That emphasis on education was a key aspect in black South African culture that enabled people there to break the bonds of apartheid and to succeed in its wake," he said.

"We need to bring this into the African-American society in Saint Louis as well. There is no drive to get it; there is no excitement, no enthusiasm," he adds. "Such a cultural change won't happen overnight, Dr. Abrahams concedes. But he said his work teaching children in Saint Louis' inner-city schools is a step in the right direction.

"That is why I am attracted to Des Lee. Des Lee is like that," Dr. Abrahams said. "What impresses me is that he actually cares about what is going on and makes the effort to interact with the people and find out what is happening. He is willing to actually put his energy in these things apart from the money he has put in, which is considerable. That's very impressive."

DR. ALLEN B. AND MRS. HELEN S. SHOPMAKER ENDOWED PROFESSORSHIP FOR EDUCATION IN COLLABORATION WITH SPRINGBOARD TO LEARNING

r. Wendy Saul was appointed to this position in August 2003. Dr. Saul works with Springboard to Learning Inc., a Saint Louis organization that provides in-school programs that break down stereotypes and broaden students' world view. Her work involves enrichment activities in the St. Louis-area primary

and secondary schools and the development of cultural, art, and science programs. She works with teacher-specialists and the Springboard staff to "motivate, stimulate and inspire" underserved children, largely in the Saint Louis Public Schools. Dr. Saul is particularly interested in helping educators create reading and writing activities that teach science and in helping students learn science from the world around them.

MORE TO COME

Other endowed professorships unfilled as of this writing, include: E. Desmond Lee Endowed Professor for Developing Women Leaders and Entrepreneurs; the E. Desmond Lee Endowed Professor For Community Collaboration and Public Policy; The Teresa M. Fischer Endowed Professorship of Citizenship Education; and the Mary Ann Lee Endowed Professor in Oncology Nursing in Connection with the Siteman Cancer Center. Dr. Xuemin "Sam" Wang, a professor of biochemistry at Kansas State University, has been hired to fill the E. Desmond Lee Endowed Professor in Plant Science in connection with the Donald Danforth Plant Science Center. The scope and nature of his work is to be defined upon his relocation to UM-St. Louis.

ALL IN THE FAMILY

Having seen the impact of Des' contributions to the community, his wife Mary Ann decided to increase her charitable giving. A woman of independent means, Mary Ann Lee has long been involved in her community in a leadership capacity, serving on the boards of John Burroughs School, Forest Park Forever, Springboard to Learning, Opera Theatre of Saint Louis, Metropolitan Association for Philanthropy and the Sheldon Theatre.

Several Saint Louis community organizations have benefited from Mary Ann's generous contributions. Her major gifts include the funds to light the King Louis statue in front of the famous Saint Louis Art Museum in Forest Park, the eight fountains in Art Lake in front of the art museum, the Des Lee Garden at the UM-St. Louis Blanche M. Touhill Performing Arts Center, the Educational Center at the Missouri Botanical

Garden and the Butterfly Wing at the Saint Louis Zoo. Most recently her generous financial support brought the Conservation Carousel to the Saint Louis Zoo. The new attraction features one-of-a-kind, hand-carved wooden animals, representing protected and endangered species at the Saint Louis Zoo.

"Kids of all ages will encounter some of the exotic animals in our collection on the carousel," says Dr. Jeffrey P. Bonner, president of the zoo. "We think this attraction, created just for us, will bring a new awareness of wildlife conservation to our young audience. The carousel will be fun, but it will also be a new way to educate children at an early age and engage families in discussion about wild animals."

"The idea of the Conservation Carousel instantly captured my interest," Mary Ann said. "I wanted this project to touch the lives of children for generations to come. I know it will be fun and educational."

From the outset, Mary Ann – mother of entrepreneur Andrew C. Taylor and Jo Ann Taylor Kindle and proud grandmother of five grandchildren – expressed her desire that economically underserved children have access to the carousel. As a result, the zoo, working through community agencies, will distribute 10,000 free tickets during the first year of operation. These tickets will also provide access to other educational exhibits at the zoo.

In addition to her charitable contributions, Mary Ann has established the Mary Ann Lee Endowed Professorship for Oncology Nursing. The professor will address the growing needs for cancer care research and the education of oncology nurses. This professor, when hired, will promote interdisciplinary research collaboration with nurses, physicians and other researchers at UM-St. Louis and with the Alvin J. Siteman Cancer Center at Washington University School of Medicine. These educators will also play an integral role in guiding student research as well as assisting in the possible establishment of a cooperative master's degree program in oncology nursing within the University of Missouri system.

Because of Mary Ann's generosity and her commitment to the St. Louis community she has been recognized with some of the regions most prrestigous awards, including. Woman of Achievement 2003, Variety Club Woman of the Year 2004, and the 2004 Hiram W. Leffingwell Award.

E. Desmond Lee Collaborative Vision at UM-St. Louis

o organization as far reaching as the DLCV runs successfully without quality people at the helm. Dr. Wendell Smith is the director of the DLCV. He is responsible for managing the organization, and his work focuses on promoting it and linking educational partners with the endowed chairs.

****

Reaching Further Into the Community

While the educational programs Des funds are near and dear to his heart, his vision for collaboration within the community extends beyond the boundaries of the academic world. For example, shortly after he established the first six endowed professorships, he announced a $2 million charitable remainder trust for the benefit of the Saint Louis Art Museum, specifically to bring outstanding exhibitions to Saint Louis

A remainder trust – in contrast to an outright, no-strings gift – provides that the donor recieves an income for his or her lifetime or the lifetime of a beneficiary. The recipient institution cannot use the trust money except as collateral during the donor's lifetime, but it becomes an outright gift after the donor's death. This document was later amended to allow the art museum to use six percent annually of the trust's proceeds, or $200 thousand a year.

"Some members of the museum's board of commissioners and trustees acknowledge that the museum has a problem with its exhibitions schedule, not only with its local audience and some benefactors, but also with its reputation in the international museum network," wrote reporter Robert Duffy in the Saint Louis Post-Dispatch.

"The museum needs an appreciation, once again, of the special rewards that come to institutions whose leaders are willing to take risks."

Des was never one to shy away from risk. That's how he built his company. And having sat at the helm of a mid-sized organization, he also recognizes the importance these types of companies play in the community. Therefore, when he accepted the Right Arm of Saint Louis award, he presented a personal challenge gift of $50 thousand to the Saint Louis Regional Chamber and Growth Association to help obtain matching resources for the establishment of a Leadership Council of 100 mid-cap company CEOs and owners.

"Our region vitally needs the potential leadership and resources of these additional mid-cap companies. Without proper leadership, we cannot hope to reach our potential. As we venture into the new millennium, it is essential that our region fully employ all its resources and capabilities. We have the talent, and it must not go to waste. Let us join forces as an expanded collaborative team to become a role model for our nation in regional problem solving."

Sitting in the audience that night was Kathy Osborn, then-vice chancellor for university relations at UM-St. Louis and a leader in launching and directing Des' educational projects at the university. Osborn had resigned from the university to become senior vice president of the RCGA. When she heard Des' challenge, she seized the opportunity. She organized the Regional Business Council of mid-cap company heads, and Des was the speaker at its first social event early in 2000.

"You are a carefully selected group of capable, successful and imaginative business entrepreneurs, CEOs and owners of our community's growing and thriving businesses," he said. "You and your companies will play a major role in the future of our region.

"The explosive technological revolution that is changing our lives will not, by itself, solve the deep-seated problems of our region. The greatest danger our community faces is standing still. Most cities decay because they don't commit themselves to change. Change is simply about leadership, ideas, values and energy. You are that leadership. Let the Regional Business Council be like the little red engine that could. If you think you can, you can."

The creation of the Regional Business Council was yet more evidence of Des' unwavering belief in the power of collaboration and partnership to enrich the quality of life in every facet of society, whether in business, education, culture or human services.

A program called the Total Quality Schools Program is another one of his funded projects. This program, offered through Washington University's John M. Olin School of Business, is an experiential learning/consulting course. Graduate and undergraduate business students work with area school leaders to identify and address issues in the school environment by using total quality management principles.

In addition, as a sustaining member of Washington University's Danforth Circle, Des has provided scholarships for deserving students who otherwise could not attend the university.

With a $500 thousand grant over 10 years, Des underwrote a program called Youth United Way. The program, which is in public and private schools, is designed to develop an appreciation for giving and to educate a new generation of leaders about the value of philanthropy in our society.

Charmaine Chapman, then-president and chief executive officer of the United Way, said "Young people will have a chance to understand why individual and corporate giving is so important for health and human services in our community."

The students will learn about philanthropy and volunteerism by raising their own money and helping decide where to spend it.

Des Lee and the Des Lee Colaborative Vision Professors

CHAPTER ELEVEN

LEADERS LEAVE THEIR MARK ON THE WORLD

"Leave your city better than you found it. If you do that, you will have done your duty."

— Ancient Greek Oath of Office

Des Lee is clearly leaving his city better than he found it, not because it is his duty, but because it is his passion. He is a complex man with dichotomies no factual recitation of his life can begin to reflect. To really understand this fascinating man, you must spend time with him, listening to his words and his sage advice. He is an idea man who worries as much about his community, his country and the world as he does about the well-being of his own family.

Des grew from a young boy to an energetic, idealistic young man, to a budding entrepreneur, to a brave soldier, to a CEO, to a compassionate philanthropist. His life is seasoned with struggles and triumphs and, most importantly, peppered with close friends, family and associates who have been rewarded by his friendship. He is a man who hopes for a better world and is willing to put himself and his money on the line to achieve that end.

This humble man wants to be remembered as a person who loved working with people and bringing out the best in them. As for being tagged with the philanthropist label, he asks, "What the hell is a philanthropist? I have no idea. I don't get up every morning and think 'I'm a philanthropist.' I don't even know what the damn word means."

He may not know what the word means, but he is one of the best. Through his charitable giving and community involvement, Des moved from being a self-described "unknown" to being a civic headliner and benefactor. Over his lifetime, his charitable giving exceeds $50 million. The April 1999 edition of Worth magazine, a financial intelligence publication, ranked him 98th among the 100 "most generous Americans" – the only Saint Louisan and one of the only two Missourians to make the list.

Perhaps, Des doesn't like the word philanthropist because he doesn't enjoy the limelight.

He'd much rather draw attention to others and give them credit for a job well done. Typically, when introducing a friend or a colleague, he spotlights their accomplishments and often remarks, "He's/she's big time."

Although he shies away from the spotlight, he likes being involved. And when Des believes in something, it's hard to stop him or even slow him down. He tackles his goals with an open wallet and the tenacity of a bulldog.

"I have asked myself many, many times, 'What are the results? What is the good? Have lives been turned around? Is our community a better place to live and work?'" he says.

The answer to those questions cannot be found in dollars and cents, numbers or statistics. They are found in the faces and the stories of the people Des has touched. The ultimate beneficiaries of Des' work are the children, senior citizens, the poor, the voiceless, the disabled – even the small-business owners struggling to make good. Most of these people he will never personally meet, but he brings them all into his philanthropic family where rhetorically there is always a warm embrace.

"I remember once when they announced the Des Lee scholarship winners at a dinner. Afterwards, Des went up to each of them and said, 'Thank you for representing me.' You could see how much that meant to them. They had been proud of winning the scholarship, but now it had a deeper meaning. He is really something special," says Dr. Judith Cochran.

Through the Collaborative Vision Des has created, he is building highways that connect people rather than walls that separate them. Even highbrow, ivory towers of academic institutions are crumbling as he erases boundaries to make campus and community strong and effective partners.

"I believe the true worth of any individual's concern for the people of this or any community is not measured so much in monuments of marble or institutions of brick and mortar, but it is in lives touched and changed," Des explains.

"When I reflect upon Des Lee's efforts," said UM-St. Louis Chancellor Emeritus Blanche M. Touhill, "I cannot help but be reminded of Henry David Thoreau, who said, 'I would give all the wealth of the world and all of the deeds of all the heroes for one true

vision.' In Saint Louis, Des Lee has provided us with that one true vision."

Some people wonder how Des Lee could give away his money. That's a legitimate question given the fact that he worked hard for what he has. He is a self-made man. Why not sit back and enjoy the fruits of his labor?

"I guess going deep sea fishing or being on the golf course all day long or traveling around the world on cruises are all good, but I believe the greatest return for me at this time is to do the type of things I am doing for the community," he says.

In his second career, Des, an octogenarian, is busier than most twenty-somethings. His calendar is filled with appointments for assistant Carole Ritter and himself. And they both love it. "I am stimulated and moved by getting to know so many wonderful people. These relationships are the greatest thing in anyone's life. I feel sorry for people who don't have the knack for communicating and connecting with people," he says.

Gayle Lee respects what her father has done. She remembers following along behind him as he walked through his old factory. She watched as he stopped to talk to every one of the company's employees, always calling them by name and asking about their families. That made an impression on her.

"This new career of his has opened up his life to a broader connection to people and allowed him to grow outside of that. The expansion of this has given him a whole new family," she says.

"He's a unique and remarkable man. He likes to pretend that he is humble and brings nothing to the table, but he is a shrewd, bright man with a clear sense of the mark he wants to make on the world," says Dr. Marvin Berkowitz.

THERE IS STILL WORK TO BE DONE

Don't talk to Des Lee about slowing down and taking it easy. While he has accomplished so much in his lifetime, there is so much more he wants to do – particularly when it comes to helping others. As long as there remains an illiterate child or one without hope or opportunity, Des' work is not finished. While Des is determined to do as much as he can, he recognizes the results of the DLCV may not become apparent for years. That's why the programs he has established are for perpetuity. Although he worries a lot about all the problems in the world, he admits he didn't assume immediate success at Lee/Rowan, and he can't assume instant success now.

"These programs are designed to continue long after my lifetime. The ills we are combating have been growing in our society for generations. They cannot be wiped out with some exotic potion or the wave of a magic wand," Des notes. "The Collaborative Vision is no magic elixir."

Des believes there are, however, certain qualities that are essential in the human experience. If we are to live in harmony with one another, we must have integrity, compassion, understanding, and respect for others. "Because of technological advances, man has been able to walk on the moon; but we have not learned to walk together in peace on earth," he adds.

"Our country is facing some of its most challenging and threatening problems. We are now engaged in a national crisis where the enemies are drugs, AIDS, alcohol addiction, decaying and deteriorating morals and family and spiritual values that are destroying the fibers of our country," he said.

"There will always be major troubles that challenge us, and people will be fighting for their own religious beliefs, their own economic future. The question is how will this world distribute its resources so that the maximum number of people will enjoy a productive, happy life. That is a problem in our community, our cities and everywhere else. Everyone wants to be happy, wants to be recognized, wants to secure certain advantages, wants to be important, wants to be appreciated, and wants to be powerful. The question is how do we develop a better economic system that will be the most advantageous for the greatest number of people. I admit I don't have the answer."

He may not have the answer. But he is determined to do his best to bring about change, and he remains confident about the future. "I realize that my efforts are like a drop of water or grain of sand, but I would rather be a drop of water or a grain of sand trying to make a difference than not doing anything."

With the tremendous amount of wealth in this country, Des is often puzzled by the fact that there are so many wealthy individuals who don't give generously to worthwhile causes. In a speech to the National Society of Fund Raising Executives, he tried to make sense of this conundrum by providing several reasons for the lack of giving.

First, he explained, "People want to keep their wealth a secret and remain very private in their lifestyle. Initially, I had intended to make my gifts anonymously. But I quickly discovered that secrets are hard to keep, and I also concluded that my giving could possibly encourage others."

Secondly, he said that he believes there is a desire to pass wealth on to the next generation to ensure a high standard of living. Additionally, he noted that many individuals are pessimistic about the future and feel as though their giving won't make a difference.

"Also, some wealthy individuals are heavily invested in privately held, family companies and trusts and are restricted in their giving. Of course, they can change that. But many have never been taught the importance and responsibility of philanthropy in improving the quality of life of their fellow man. They just don't get it," he says.

Last, but not least, Des notes that many wealthy people have no idea of the personal satisfaction, joy, fulfillment and gratification that can result from giving to worthy causes. "There is nothing more rewarding," he notes.

HANGING ONTO THE AMERICAN DREAM

Des Lee epitomizes the American Dream. A self-made man, he knows the challenges and the rewards of building a business and the importance of the free enterprise system.

"There is no system I know of anywhere in the world as great as our free enterprise system. It challenges people to think," he explains.

However, the system is not without its flaws, and Des is concerned about the current business climate in which there has been a deterioration of trust.

"You are either honest, or you aren't. Humility and integrity are probably the greatest single qualities in managing any business, whether it is a two- or three-man operation or thousands of men," he notes.

Despite moments of discouragement, Des continues to believe in the American Dream. "I never want to give up hope. I want to be on the side of trying. America began as a country of liberated people who came here for freedom. There are many success stories. Our country was built on drive.

"A few of my friends say to me that our grandchildren won't have the same opportunities that we had. That may be true, but I don't believe it. We have far too many wonderful assets in our community, consisting of spiritual, cultural, educational, medical, business and civic organizations that represent our rich heritage, to be pessimistic about our future."

Des is a deep thinker and his astute observations about our society and our economic system are noteworthy. He firmly believes that we are living on the threshold of the greatest period of enlightenment the world has known and that we are all very fortunate to be a free people and to be able to enjoy the opportunities this affords us. The free enterprise system, he opines, is the best way to stimulate growth and to provide advantages and the highest standard of living for our society.

"But," he cautions, "the corporate world is getting, unfortunately, too bottom-line oriented. The leaders have been so highly compensated in many cases and their compensation has become out of balance with the working man and woman. They've gotten a lot of bad press. I think the corporate leadership is going to have to improve that picture. One of the great dangers in this environment will be the de-emphasis on social values and the importance of people.

"As long as we have a sickness in our urban areas – people who are not fully participating and feeling they are left out – there is no hope. You can't have happiness and a healthy society unless you correct the infection.

"I firmly believe that if we are to maximize the quality of life that the future offers, we must find a way to preserve the dignity and the self-esteem of the individual. We must never lose our faith and hope in the future.

"My philosophy for making the community a better place for all of us is to encourage and inspire collaboration and partnerships that can produce a synergy far exceeding the efforts of any one segment working independently."

Des Lee

Young Des Lee

Chapter Twelve

In His Own Words

Des sums up his philosophy and his work in his own words: "I never thought I would ever be the subject of a book written about me and my activities. I feel that my professors are outstanding, talented, intelligent and committed individuals who have formed a team with special skills to make the Saint Louis region a better place to live and an expanded opportunity for its children. It is my hope that this unique collaboration will grow stronger and increasingly more effective in its mission as it lives in perpetuity.

"The collaboration is a symbol for diversity in our ever-changing world that presents challenges to our culture. It is also my hope that the Des Lee Collaborative Vision will become a role model for other communities, their universities, their cultural, business, governmental and educational organizations.

"I am indebted to all those wonderful visionary individuals who have encouraged me to build and formulate this collaboration. That includes Mary Ann, my wife; Carole Ritter, my administrative associate; Dr. Blanche Touhill, Chancellor Emeritus of the University of Missouri-Saint Louis; Dr. William Danforth, Chancellor/Chairman Emeritus of Washington University; Dr. Mark Wrighton, Chancellor of Washington University; Dr. Richard Meyers, President of Webster University; Dr. Karen Luebbert, Vice President, Webster University; and Kathy Osborn, Executive Director of the Regional Business Council.

These and many other individuals with whom I have had the pleasure of working have guided my efforts and provided me with strength, courage and determination.

"I also wish to extend my deepest thanks to my family. It is not surprising that all three of my children – Gayle, Gary, and Christy – are totally different in their personalities, aptitudes and interests. Yet, they fully support the work we are doing with the Collaborative Vision.

"Gayle is more introverted, a deep thinker, extremely sensitive and finds fulfillment in *helping handicapped individuals improve the quality of their lives and strengthen their hope. Gayle feels blessed to have an autistic daughter, Lyrica.*

"Gary is extremely extroverted and probably one of the greatest salesmen you will ever meet. He is very kind and sensitive along with possessing a drive and unquenchable determination that will let him open almost any door. Gary's daughter, Elizabeth, runs a specialty clothing store, and his son, David, is a basketball player recruited by several major NCAA college teams and is now captain at the University of Florida in Gainesville.

"Christy is, likewise, extremely extroverted, determined and persevering along with having a bubbly, fun-loving personality. She is also an "unlocker" of doors as she has been able to sell expensive art that the average salesman would never be able to do. After going broke in two small art galleries, she has developed a tremendous business with very expensive art. She has one son Desmond, a well-rounded kid who is a good problem solver. I am richly blessed to have four unique, fine grandchildren, of whom I am very proud.

"All three of my children posses good athletic genes, which they probably inherited from their mother and, perhaps, a little from their father. I am proud of each of them and their individuality. My love for them is returned many-fold by their love and acceptance of me and my life. This is also true in their relationship with their mother, Margery.

"Beyond my family, this collaboration is unique because it brings together extremely talented professors whose expertise touches all major areas of our community. It provides them an opportunity to work together sharing their skills, philosophies and energies. One of its greatest strengths is the unselfishness and caring on the part of all its partners as they strive to build a better community. I can only hope that my dream and commitment will leave its mark in history as the collaboration becomes stronger and continues to touch lives at all levels in perpetuity."

PROLOGUE

Des Lee is a man who stands above the rest. Not because of his six-foot-four-inch stature, but because of his vision, his compassion and his integrity. He is a man of uncompromising values, a rarity in a culture plagued with dishonesty.

He is a wealthy man, not because his bank account puts him among society's elite, but because of the value of his many friends. His treasure consists of the people he knows and the people whose lives he has touched. Measured in those terms, it is hard to imagine a richer man.

Having had the honor and the privilege of getting to know this uncommon man as the author of this book and to introduce him to you, the reader, has been a rich experience for me. "Thank you, Des, for being a role model and an inspiration to us all. My life is certainly richer for having shared a part of yours."

Susan Wilson Solovic